MW00936580

GOLD NUGGETS FROM God's Mine

366 Daily Devotional

Denise Smith-Lewis

WestBow Press books may be ordered through booksellers or by contacting:

WestBow Press
A Division of Thomas Nelson & Zondervan
1663 Liberty Drive
Bloomington, IN 47403
www.westbowpress.com
844-714-3454

ISBN: 978-1-6642-3303-4 (sc)
ISBN: 978-1-6642-3302-7 (hc)
ISBN: 978-1-6642-3304-1 (e)

Library of Congress Control Number: 2021908747

Print information available on the last page.

WestBow Press rev. date: 10/19/2021

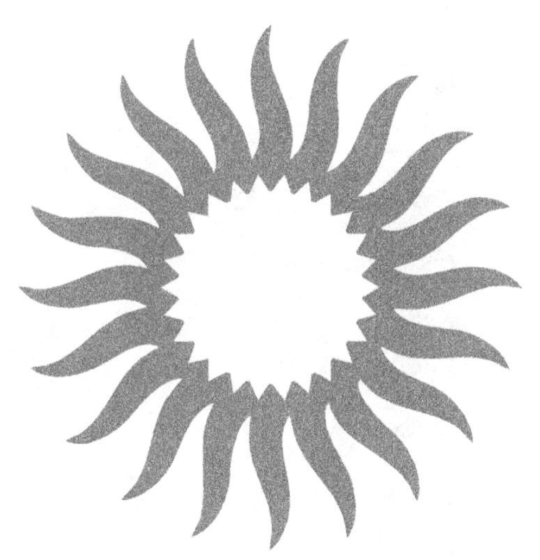

Acknowledgments

My praise and thanksgiving belong to almighty God whose goodness and mercy remain my ambassadorial escorts and supernatural security. My access to this Christ resource enabled me to complete this project.

The project *Gold Nuggets from God's Mine* began a long time ago. There were some mishaps that led to seasons of discouragement and delays. Today, I celebrate God's grace that brought it to fruition.

I offer my profound thanks to those who supported me along the journey.

To Kelah Joseph, thank you for your labor of love. To the Rev. Nasel Ephraim, Rev. Elva Richards-Goodwin, Bernadine Philip, Jamilla Connor, Holliette Valentine, Leunda Callendar, and Ted Martin, thank you for the part you played. To the Rt. Rev. Dr. Conrad Spencer and to all who partnered with me in this project, my heartfelt appreciation. To my husband, children, and other members of my family, thank you for your love and support. To every reader, I pray you will be enriched in every way by these gold nuggets. Do enjoy your gold-mining experience.

1

I Am Eternally Loved!

I have loved you, my people, with an everlasting love.
With unfailing love, I have drawn you to myself.
JEREMIAH 31:3 (NLT)

I don't have to measure up, perform, or be perfect to receive God's love. God loves me unconditionally, fully, and completely.

God loves me with my insecurities and inadequacies, my faults and my failings. He loves me and accepts me just as I am. I am complete in God's love. Therefore, I accept myself and love myself as I am. Thank you, Lord, for this love. Amen.

I have nothing to prove.
I am worthy of God's love.

2

God Thinks Good Thoughts!

"For I know the plans I have for you," declares the Lord, "plans to prosper you and not to harm you, plans to give you hope and a future."
JEREMIAH 29:11 (NIV)

Did you know that God thinks highly of you and that God favors you? He does. From the bowels of eternity, God made plans for your future, a future filled with hope and success.

Amid the challenges you experience today, remember that God is working on your future to make it good. Rest assured, tomorrow will be better. Simply trust him. Thank you, Lord. With you, my future looks good. Amen.

Lord, here is my life's plan,
my today and my tomorrows.
I place them in your hands.

3

God's Resources Are Limitless

With God are wisdom and might; he has counsel and understanding.

JOB 12:13 (ESV)

Everything belongs to God: infinite wisdom, unlimited power, perfect knowledge, and pure love. There is no shortage, there is no scarcity, and there is no lack with God. Whatever I need, God has it in stock. His storehouse is always full.

Whenever I have a need, I only have to ask, and God makes every resource of heaven available to me. I ask. and I receive it! God, owner of all that is, give all I need. Amen.

Whenever I cry, God will supply.

4

Made to Rule

Then God said, "Let us make man in our image,
after our likeness. And let them have dominion
over the fish of the sea … and all the earth."
GENESIS 1:26 (ESV)

God fashioned us like himself, in his image and likeness. He formed us from the substance with which he is made and breathed his breath into us. He gave us the capacity to function as he does and appointed us as the CEO of his creation.

Being God's CEO is a privilege and an awesome responsibility. We must exercise our dominion with dignity, authority, grace, and humility. God is expecting us to manage well. Help us live up to our potential, Lord. Amen.

Friend, you have greatness
on the inside of you.
Now do the things God wants you to.

5

God Can Do It

Is anything too hard for the Lord? I will return about this time next year, and Sarah will have a son.

GENESIS 18:14 (NLT)

The sovereign God who holds supreme power is never hindered by obstacles. He knows no setbacks and no limitations, and he is certainly not restrained by boundaries or borders. Sarah and Abraham were past childbearing age, but God reversed the irreversible and gave them a son.

No matter the degree of difficulty, God can handle your case. Do not think your situation is too great or too impossible for him. God is up to the challenge. Be expectant, and you will be triumphant. God can do it. Amen.

No matter the difficulty,
God gives victory!

Rise above Words!

David was now in great danger ... and they began to talk of stoning him. But David found strength in the Lord his God.

1 SAMUEL 30:6 (NLT)

Threatening words can become a source of distress for anyone. They did for David. He overcame this negative situation by finding strength in God's Word.

Like David, you will face difficult moments when harsh and discouraging words are spoken to you. Create a "trash file" for people's negative words; then remember God's words to you. Go on. Encourage yourself in the Lord and rise above words! Lord, give me ears for you only. Amen.

Learn to lean on the Lord and
make yourself strong with God's Word.

7

Living Purposefully

For if you remain silent at this time, relief and deliverance for the Jews will arise ... And who knows but that you have come to your royal position for such a time as this?

ESTHER 4:14 (NIV)

Little orphan Esther, who was raised by her uncle Mordecai, became the queen of the Persian Empire. She fulfilled her life's purpose by helping to deliver her people, the Jewish people.

Do you know why you were born? Here's the reason: you were born to serve God in this season. So take the time to discover how you can, with courage, live purposefully. Lord, this is our prayer: help us know why we are here. Amen.

Do not waste your time.
Count every opportunity as prime.

8

Holy Hiding

No one is holy like the Lord! There is no one besides you; there is no Rock like our God.

1 SAMUEL 2:2 (NLT)

When it comes to holiness, righteousness, and faithfulness, God is in a class all by himself. There is no one like him, no one who can be compared to him, and no one who is equal to him. God is total safety and total security. He is a shelter in the storm and shade in the heat.

When storms come against us, let us take up his offer and run behind this rock for cover. He will protect us and keep us safe. Hide us, Lord, on this day. Amen.

In our rock, take cover;
he will secure us forever.

9

God Will Appear

But—when God our Savior revealed his kindness and love, he saved us, not because of the righteous things we had done, but because of his mercy.

TITUS 3:4–5 (NLT)

God's mercy does not depend on who we are or on what we have done but upon God, who is always willing to show mercy. This is awesome! It is incredible to think that God's mercy will show up whenever we need it.

We are assured today that wherever we are, whatever our situation is, God's love and his mercy will appear. Thank you, Lord, for showing us your kindness. Amen.

God is kind.
His mercies you will find.

10

Watch Your Mouth!

Show yourself in all respects to be a model of good works, and in your teaching show integrity, dignity, and sound speech that cannot be condemned, so that an opponent may be put to shame, having nothing evil to say about us.

TITUS 2:7–8 (ESV)

Too many times, we engage in loose and lewd speech. During those times, we are poor witnesses of our faith, and we fail to model Christ. Let us be good examples and practice sound speech that lifts others.

We should always check the sound of our speech before we speak. If it is not uplifting, it should not be heard. It matters what we say. Lord, help us to use our mouths to bring your glory out. Amen.

Watch what you say.
Be an example and lead the way.

11

God Remembers

And a book of remembrance was written before him of those who feared the Lord and esteemed his name.

MALACHI 3:16 (ESV)

Human memory tends to deteriorate with age and traumatic experiences, but we can count on God to remember.

God takes note of all we do in honor of his name. He creates a book of remembrance where our actions, though unrecognized by others, will never be forgotten by him.

God sees every good deed we have done, and he remembers. When our actions are motivated by our love for God and the honor of his name, he takes notice. Thank you, Lord, for taking notice of us. Amen.

Good deeds do not bring fame,
but they certainly make God
remember our name.

12

God Is Calling You

"Come follow me," Jesus said, "and I will send you out to fish for people."

MATTHEW 4:19 (NIV)

Christ walked beside the Sea of Galilee and found Peter and others whom he had sent to fish for people. Christ walks beside the sea of our lives every day. In low and high tides, he is there. He comes alongside us and teaches us to come alongside others.

As we follow in obedience to Jesus, we learn to journey with others as he journeys with us. It is wonderful. Help us to follow you, Lord. Amen.

This is evidence of God's faithfulness;
God invites us into greatness.

13

In Search of One

If a man owns a hundred sheep, and one of them wanders away, will he not leave the ninety-nine on the hills and go to look for the one that wandered off?

MATTHEW 18:12 (NIV)

Each one of us has value and significance to God, and he treasures a relationship with us. When we go astray, this relationship is interrupted and our communion is broken. God leaves heaven and comes in search of us over valleys and rocky mountains.

Yes, he puts everything on hold until he finds us. He will rest only when we return to the safety and security of his arms. We are important to God and worth the search. Thank you, God, for searching for us. Amen.

People, we are worthy;
we are God's number one priority.

14

Learn to Love

Love never ends. As for prophecies, they will pass away; as for tongues, they will cease; as for knowledge, it will pass away.

1 CORINTHIANS 13:8 (ESV)

God's love is like the ocean, endless and boundless. And God's love is available to us in totality. We will never be in a situation where God's love cannot reach us.

God's love never fails. People and things will fail. We will fail, but God's love never fails, never runs out, and never falls out. It is so comforting to know that no matter what fails, God's love will always prevail. Wrap us in your love, Lord. Amen.

When all else fails,
God's love still prevails.

15

Confessing Is Right

If we confess our sins, he is faithful and just to forgive us our sins and to cleanse us from all unrighteousness.

1 JOHN 1:9 (ESV)

Keeping unconfessed sin in our hearts is like keeping garbage in our homes. After a while, it begins to putrefy and contaminate our lives, producing sickness and disease.

Confession, however, cleanses the soul, covers our sin, and makes us whole. Confession helps us yield to God's control, giving us the grace to be courageous and bold. Confession opens the door of forgiveness, and we walk free and without condemnation. Hear our confession, Lord. We are sorry. Amen.

Confession for sure
will lead to a soul cure.

16

Good Foundation

They are like a man building a house, who dug down deep and laid the foundation on the rock. When a flood came, the torrent struck that house but could not shake it, because it was well built.

LUKE 6:48 (NIV)

The priority of any house is the foundation. A proper foundation ensures the house can withstand the forces of time and weather.

When the foundation of our lives is built on God's Word—faith, love, integrity, sincerity, righteousness, joy, and peace—we, too, can weather the storms of life. Let's make God our sure foundation. We will outlast the storms. Master builder, help us to build wisely. Amen.

Let this be our goal and aspiration.
God is our sure foundation.

17

Let Your Mouth Speak Good Things

Out of the same mouth come praise and cursing.
My brothers and sisters, this should not be.

JAMES 3:10 (NIV)

It is not unusual to hear a person speak words of praise one moment and then use words that curse the next moment. Our mouths, as with every other facet of life, hold the propensity for good or evil, blessings and cursing.

James challenges us to change this anomaly. We must use our mouths for praising and not murmuring, for blessing and not cursing. Develop a daily practice to speak blessings over people's lives! Lord, let our mouths bless you and build others. Amen.

When we use our mouths to bless,
we give others rest.

18

Blessings Follow Obedience

"If you walk in my statutes and observe my commandments and do them, then I will give you your rains in their season, and the land shall yield its increase … And you shall eat your bread to the full and dwell in your land securely."

LEVITICUS 26:3–5 (ESV)

Scripture is replete with the encouragement to obey. Obedience is the key that opens the door of blessings. Prosperity in the land, security, and peace at our borders are some of the wonderful blessings of obedience.

These blessings are available to us and are activated when we keep God's commands. Today, let us obey God's laws and commands and be at peace in the land. Write your laws on our hearts, Lord. Amen.

Let your obedience show.
Then the blessings will flow.

19

God Stands

Then the angel of the Lord stood at a place where the road narrowed between two vineyard walls.

NUMBERS 22:24 (NLT)

When our ways are contrary, driven by disobedience, relished by rebellion, and energized by envy, God stands in our way. He sent his angel and stood in Balaam's way.

God stands in our way to prevent us from hurting ourselves and others. When we turn from following his commands, when we are tempted by sin, when we forget to pray and are tempted to go astray, God comes before us and stands in the way. Thank you, Lord, for standing in our way. Amen.

God, if we are tempted
to do wrong this day,
please come and stand in our way.

20

When God goes Slowly

The LORD is slow to anger, abounding in love, and forgiving sin and rebellion.

NUMBERS 14:18 (NIV)

When God deals with us, he is always patient. He is never angry, emotional, or irrational, and sometimes he seems to go slowly. Remember he is making it possible for his mercy and grace to show. He is simply taking the time to clear the obstacles on our path so that his blessings of love and forgiveness can flow. Lord, give us patience and wisdom to know when you are *going slowly.* Amen.

Remember when God goes slowly,
his love and mercy show clearly.

21

God Is For You

Whenever the Lord raised up a judge over Israel,
he was with that judge and rescued the people from
their enemies throughout the judge's lifetime.

JUDGES 2:18 (NLT)

God is our deliverer. He can use anyone and anything as his instrument of deliverance. God raised judges to deliver his people. He used animals, trees, and seas to save his people from their enemies.

God's delivering ability has not diminished. God still delivers, and he will deliver us today. The Lord knows the details and the circumstances, and he will give the deliverance. Thank you for deliverance, Lord. Amen.

God has unmatched abilities;
he specializes in deliverance
from enemies.

22

What Is Your Position?

She would sit under the Palm of Deborah … and the Israelites would go to her for judgment.

JUDGES 4:5 (NLT)

God called Deborah to a position of serving as a judge of Israel. Her court of justice was under a palm tree. She kept her position and was faithful in service.

We, too, are called to a position of service. Like Deborah, we need to remain focused and faithful in the place where God has called us. It may not be a popular place or an easy place, but it is our assigned place. So serve with diligence. Serve with excellence. Help us, Lord, to do so. Amen.

Today, we make the decision
to maintain our position.

23

God Is Good Refuge

The Lord repay you for what you have done, and a full reward is given to you by the Lord, the God of Israel, under whose wings you have come to take refuge!

RUTH 2:12 (ESV)

Ruth and Naomi found themselves alone except for each other. Without help and hope, they sought and found refuge in God.

The best place to seek refuge is under God. No one can impeach him, unseat him, unsettle him, dethrone him, or defeat him. This was Ruth and Naomi's experience. He became their provider and defender. Under God, we have full coverage. If God is our refuge, we are in good hands; we are in God's hands. God, we thank you for keeping us safe. Amen.

Rest under God's wing.
It is a good covering.

24

When You Give, You Get

"May the Lord give you children by this woman to take the place of the one she prayed for and gave to the Lord." … And the Lord was gracious to Hannah; she gave birth to three sons and two daughters.

1 SAMUEL 2:20–21 (NIV)

Hannah, like many women, experienced difficulty conceiving. She promised God that if he enabled her to have a son, she would give her son back to him. She did. Hannah did not count her only son too much to give to God.

God was moved by Hannah's generosity. He rewarded her with five children after Samuel. From God's touch, Hannah received much. So give your best to God, and he will give you better than your best. We can never outgive God. Lord, free us to give. Amen.

Generous giver, we give.
It's the best way to live.

25

Don't Compromise on You

He did what was pleasing in the Lord's sight,
just as his ancestor David had done.
2 CHRONICLES 29:2 (NLT)

Hezekiah had many decisions to make as Israel's king. He chose to follow his ancestor David, doing what was right in God's sight.

Doing the right should not depend on who is looking. We should do the right because it is right and pleasing in God's sight. If we live with the awareness that we are in God's sight, we will seek to do what is right. Remember, God is a present and personal audience who examines and judges our actions, thoughts, and intentions. Lord, help us to do right in your sight. Amen.

Always do the right,
regardless of who is insight.

26

Keep Dreaming

Pharaoh said to Joseph, "I hereby put you in charge of the entire land of Egypt."
GENESIS 41:41 (NLT)

God gave Joseph big dreams for his life. His brothers' jealousy landed him in the pit. Potiphar's wife's lies landed him in the prison, but God's favor landed him in the palace. Joseph could have given up over the many years of trials from the pit to the palace. He kept on dreaming, believing, and hoping.

Don't be disheartened when you face difficult circumstances. God is in control. Hold on to this assurance. Hold on to your dreams. One day you will reach the palace. Lord, help us hold to your promise and hope in you. Amen.

Delays are not denials.
Keep dreaming.
Your breakthrough is coming.

27

God Has Answered

Then let us arise and go up to Bethel, so that I may make there an altar to the God who answers me in the day of my distress and has been with me wherever I have gone.

GENESIS 35:3 (ESV)

Jacob practiced deception, which hurt members of his family and led him to a time of distress. When he cried to God for help, God answered and brought him relief and release. Jacob went to Bethel to offer his thanks and praise.

It is time to build an altar and give praise to God. He has brought us through difficult moments, even those of our own making. Like Jacob, we need to express gratitude to the God who is true, the God who brought us through. God, we thank you, that when we call you answer. Bless the Lord! Amen.

Let us cry to God in times of distress.
God will answer, and we'll be blessed.

28

Shepherd All My Life

And he blessed Joseph and said, "The God before whom my fathers Abraham and Isaac walked, the God who has been my shepherd all my life to this day."

GENESIS 48:15 (ESV)

Jacob was old and nearing death. In the process of speaking a blessing on his children, he acknowledged God's provision all his life. So can we.

Like Jacob, we affirm God has been our shepherd. Every day of our lives, we are loved, cared for, sheltered, protected, comforted, guided, and healed. What a privilege! God supplies all our needs. We thank you, God, for your provision and protection. Thank you, Lord, for shepherding our lives. Amen.

God is a shepherd. I affirm it is true,
and I know God will shepherd you.

29

Stay at It

But again Elisha replied, "As surely as the Lord lives and you yourself live, I will never leave you." So they went on together.

2 KINGS 2:6 (NLT)

Elisha served Elijah under many and varying circumstances: when it was easy and when it was not easy. Elisha chose to stay even when others discouraged him. He did not leave Elijah. He served him until God separated them.

Relationships require work. The task of loving and caring for others is a demanding one, and sometimes we may want out of the relationship. We desire to leave because it is no longer convenient to stay. Let us challenge ourselves to stay and resist the temptation to walk away. Lord, help us to go on with our brothers and sisters. Amen.

God, give us fortitude
and a good work attitude.

30

Command the Morning

"Have you ever commanded the morning to appear and caused the dawn to rise in the east?"

JOB 38:12 (NLT)

God commanded the morning of creation. He called for light out of the darkness and order out of chaos. He ensured that the day was filled with his divine agenda.

We, too, can infuse our day with divine blessings. We do not have to allow the morning to come with any surprises. There is power in our words, so let us command today. This day shall be filled with favor, grace, and blessings. This day shall bring peace, light, and power to do the right. Amen and amen.

Commanding the morning
is the right way
to bring order to your day.

31

All God's

The earth is the Lord's and the fullness thereof,
the world and those who dwell therein.

PSALM 24:1 (ESV)

We possess so many things: houses, land, money. Yet we own nothing, for it all belongs to the Lord.

We are simply stewards who must give an account of the resources God has placed in our hands. The truth is we have them for only a season. Therefore, let us use God's gifts with integrity, dignity, and humility. Help us to manage with wisdom, Lord, remembering they all belong to you. Amen.

Hold God's possessions loosely;
they are not yours truly.

32

Mouthguard

I said, "I will guard my ways, that I may not sin with my tongue; I will guard my mouth with a muzzle, so long as the wicked are in my presence."

PSALM 39:1 (ESV)

The psalmist decided to pay attention to his thoughts to avoid sinning with his tongue. He determined to go to the extreme and muzzle his mouth in the presence of wicked people.

Like him, we must be careful with our words. We must guard what comes from our mouths, mindful that our words may be used to snare and destroy us. Guarding our mouths means knowing when to keep quiet and when to speak. May God give us the wisdom to know the difference. If wisdom doesn't work, try a muzzle. Help us, Lord. Amen.

When sound speech is hard,
try a mouthguard.

33

Love Does Not Leave

"Don't ask me to leave you and turn back. Wherever you go, I will go; wherever you live, I will live."
RUTH 1:16 (NLT)

Blinded, broken, and bewildered by grief, Naomi encouraged Ruth to return to her Moabite family. Ruth's love was able to distinguish between Naomi's voice and Naomi's need. Naomi's heart needed companionship and love, so Ruth stayed.

God offers us a love that does not leave us in moments of brokenness. It stays and offers us healing and hope. Love builds us up and gives us the capacity to cope. Thank you for the love that never leaves us. Amen.

Real love stays.
Real love is coming your way.

34

Wait

I waited patiently for the LORD; he turned to me and heard my cry.

PSALM 40:1 (NIV)

David's testimony of answered prayer is encouraging. David called out to God, and God listened to his distress cry. David waited for God to respond, and God answered.

Today we are encouraged not to be quick to move but willing to wait. Remember God needs some time to hear us and then to answer. We call; God listens, God hears, and God responds. Between our calling and God's responding, there is a period of waiting. Increase our capacity for waiting, Lord. Amen.

Call earnestly.
God is waiting patiently.

35

Quiet Confidence

In quietness and trust shall be your strength.

ISAIAH 30:15 (ESV)

In times of trouble, it is easy to be fearful and full of flurry. Fear and flurry, however, only weaken us and make us more afraid. In these moments, we need to place our trust in God, recognizing that our God is bigger than our problem, and simply be quiet. Our quietness may be mistaken for weakness, but it may just be our strength working undercover. Remember the adage *don't judge the book by its cover.*

The truth is when you know where your strength lies and who your strength is, you can afford to keep quiet. Keep us still, Lord. Amen.

Stillness is not a weakness.

36

Pray On

Elijah was a man with a nature like ours, and he prayed fervently that it might not rain, and for three years and six months, it did not rain on the earth.

JAMES 5:17 (ESV)

Elijah was a man who showed strength and weakness, courage and cowardice, faith and fear. That sounds like us, right? Yet he had success at prayer, and so can we.

Prayer is not prevented by our weakness but made possible through God's greatness. The biggest part of the prayer is the one who hears. He will hear you; he will hear me. Thank you for hearing us, O Lord. Amen.

Earnest prayer
always catches God's ear.

37

God Is Good

"Give thanks to the Lord of Heaven's Armies, for the Lord is good. His faithful love endures forever!"
JEREMIAH 33:11 (NLT)

Jeremiah was persecuted for his prophetic stance. Through hard times, he made the startling discovery that God is total goodness. His loving-kindness endures forever. Because God is faithful, Jeremiah's only recourse was to give thanks.

You, too, can make your evaluation. The truth will startle you. God is faithful. So, bask in his love, his kindness, his goodness, and his grace, knowing that they never run out, and then give thanks. That's all you can do. Thank you, Lord. Amen.

We live by God's grace.
His kindness we trace.

38

Supernatural Security

Surely your goodness and love will follow me all the days of my life.

PSALM 23:6 (NIV)

God's goodness and loving-kindness follow us everywhere we go. They continually chase after us. Many can recall being chased by something threatening like a dog. Many have also tried to escape the path of a tornado. It is a different experience to be chased by something wonderful like goodness and mercy.

We can only feel secure with ambassadorial escorts like goodness and mercy. Because of them, we are afforded a dwelling in God's house forever. So, let us enjoy our diplomatic status. Remember who we are representing. Lord, we surely thank you. Amen.

Goodness and mercy are good companions continually.

39

Word of Honor

I would no more reject my people than I would change my laws that govern night and day, earth and sky.

JEREMIAH 33:25 (NLT)

Some things do last forever. God's covenant and his Word do. God has made some promises he cannot repent, relent, or recant. His word is as good as gold; well, it is better.

What is his covenant with you? God promises to be your God and to care for you as his child. He will be your shield and defender, your rock of refuge. God promises to bring you through every situation, and he will. He always keeps his word of honor. Lord, we trust you wholly and take you at your word. Amen.

God's Word and covenant are true.
God will take care of you.

40

Take Warning

"Son of man, I have appointed you as a watchman for Israel. Whenever you receive a message from me, warn people immediately."

EZEKIEL 3:17 (NLT)

Ezekiel was appointed as God's watchman. When he heard God speak, he had the responsibility to warn God's people.

A warning can seem like an interruption or intrusion and may not always be appreciated. Sometimes it may even be rejected and regarded as offensive. God appointed us as watchmen in the land to warn others. Our appointment is both a privilege and a responsibility. Whether the people accept or reject us, we must deliver the message. Give us discerning ears to hear you, Lord, and hearts to obey. Amen.

Do your task diligently.
Warn God's people faithfully.

41

Live

"And when I passed by you and saw you wallowing in your blood, I said to you in your blood, 'Live!' I said to you in your blood, 'Live!'"

EZEKIEL 16:6 (ESV)

Jehovah-El Roi, the God who sees, took notice of you in your helpless, hopeless situation. He saw you when the circumstances threatened to destroy you. And when you were wallowing in death, God saw you and spoke life to you.

Your present situation may be discouraging, dicey, dismal, and filled with despair. The odds seem stacked against you, and you feel death is near. Do not fear. God's word to you today is live. You will make it today. You will live. Thank you, Lord. Amen.

Live and let live.

42

Quite a Spread

I spread the corner of my garment over you and covered your naked body. I gave you my solemn oath and entered into a covenant with you, declares the Sovereign LORD, and you became mine.

EZEKIEL 16:8 (NIV)

The experiences of life have a way of uncovering our vulnerabilities and exposing us to shame and ridicule. It seems like we are an onion stripped down to the core. In those moments, we are weak and fragile. God, however, takes the initiative; he covers us and covenants with us.

Take heart, friend. God is covering you right now. God's skirt is not simply for decoration but for protection, provision, pardon, peace, and the prolonging of your life. God will cover your pain and shame. Ah, Lord, cover us. Amen.

The God who is on the throne
covers his own.

43

Requirements

He has shown you, O mortal, what is good. And what does the LORD require of you? To act justly and to love mercy and to walk humbly with your God.

MICAH 6:8 (NIV)

God requires us to do justice, love mercy, and walk humbly with him. This, God states, is the whole duty of our human living. This means we are called to reflect God's nature and character in our relationships.

How do we do this? We must be fair in our dealings with others. We must treat them the way we want them to treat us. We must do our duty and do it well. Remember, when we walk humbly with God, we walk with honor among all. Help us walk well, Lord. Amen.

When we love mercy,
we will walk humbly.

44

Put Together

I will surely assemble all of you, O Jacob; I will gather the remnant of Israel; I will set them together like sheep in a fold.

MICAH 2:12 (ESV)

When pieces of a puzzle are missing, they never give a complete picture. So, when pieces of our lives are scattered, we can never be complete or whole. Scattered pieces can also get lost and lose their value and effectiveness. God is aware of this principle, so he makes the promise: "I will gather you."

Your brokenness cannot last in the presence of God's completeness. God delights in putting together broken pieces and making them a complete whole. You are at God's assembly line. It is now your turn. Pray, "Fix me, Jesus. Amen."

Broken?
Come to God's fold.
You will be mended and made whole.

45

Spirit-Filled

But as for me, I am filled with power—with the Spirit of the Lord. I am filled with justice and strength.

MICAH 3:8 (NLT)

Living in this world is challenging and, I dare say, difficult. God fortifies me in four different ways: I am filled with God's power, with God's Spirit, with justice, and with courage. I am not easily shaken. I cannot but make it.

When God fills us with his resources, we will be successful. If you allow God to fill you, you will be successful too. Lord, we commit our lives to you. Amen.

God has equipped you
with super-four power for the hour.

46

What's on Your Head?

Those the LORD has rescued will return. They will enter Zion with singing; everlasting joy will crown their heads. Gladness and joy will overtake them, and sorrow and sighing will flee away.

ISAIAH 51:11 (NIV)

I remember as a child carrying buckets of water on my head. It felt as if every part of me was being dragged down. But God lifted my head and filled me with his joy.

Many people carry worry and problems they deem insurmountable on their heads. God, however, lifts our heads and gives us everlasting joy to carry instead. I urge us to carry joy. Crown our heads with joy, Lord. Amen.

Be spirit led
and carry joy on your head.

47

Let's Exchange

"Come now, let's settle this," says the Lord. "Though your sins are like scarlet, I will make them as white as snow. Though they are red like crimson, I will make them as white as wool."

ISAIAH 1:18 (NLT)

In God's courtroom, God is judge, defender, prosecutor, and juror. We are, however, assured of a fair trial. Our case is never prejudiced.

In God's court, we come already guilty because of the overwhelming evidence of our sins. God, the just judge, takes our guilty plea. When we admit guilt, he cancels it and clears us of all wrongdoing. God declares we are free. What an exchange! Lord, hear my plea. I am guilty. Have mercy on me. Amen.

I am no longer guilty.
I am pardoned justified and free!

48

Still Here

For the upright will live in the land, and
the blameless will remain in it.
PROVERBS 2:21 (NIV)

Any honest evaluation or reflection on life will lead to the conclusion *God is good*. He has preserved us amid many attempts and threats to our lives. We came close to destruction, but because of his goodness, we are still here in the land of the living.

Look back over the way you have come, the trials and the tribulations. You may have been abused and misused, but you are still here. You have been persecuted and accused, but you are still here. And you will remain here because God declared it to be so. Praise be to God, who keeps his promise. Amen.

Praise God for his mercy and care.
I am still here.

49

Uninterrupted Power

Abide in me, and I in you. As the branch cannot bear fruit by itself, unless it abides in the vine, neither can you, unless you abide in me.

JOHN 15:4 (ESV)

If we have hope of maximizing our potential and simply bearing fruit, we must abide in Jesus. Yes, we must obey Jesus's word of command. We must stay connected and have communion with our God, who is our power source.

When we remain plugged into the source, we have access to an uninterrupted power supply, which allows us to produce and bear fruit. We will be a benefit and a blessing to others. We will be excellent transmitters who are empowered to change our world. Help us, Lord, Amen.

Stay connected to the source,
and transmit with accurate force.

50

From Good Stock

I praise you, for I am fearfully and wonderfully made.
PSALM 139:14 (ESV)

What an awesome God we serve! He does not make mistakes. He is excellent in all his ways, and he made me simply beautiful. Yes, God does all things well.

I am not like anyone else. I am God's unique masterpiece. I was crafted by the hand of the Master with exquisite and expensive material. I am from good stock. Therefore, I will walk away from the negative opinions of people and remember who I am, God's gem. Lord, remind me who I am. Amen.

God accepts you the way you are—
a beauty, a gem, a star.

51

Letting Go

No, dear brothers and sisters, I have not achieved it, but I focus on this one thing: Forgetting the past and looking forward to what lies ahead.

PHILIPPIANS 3:13 (NLT)

The apostle Paul undoubtedly was one of the greatest Christian leaders. Reflecting on his life, he concluded that though he had come a long way, he still had far to go—more people to reach, more people to teach.

Like Paul, I am not there yet. I can only get ahead when I let go of things of the past. So today, I make my decision. I will let go, Lord, and look ahead. I let them go in your hand. Amen.

Lord, I let them go.
Let your peace flow.

52

Prayer Nonstop

Never stop praying.

1 THESSALONIANS 5:17 (NLT)

Prayer is powerful. Through prayer, the apostle Paul experienced great victories and fulfilled the purposes of God in his life. We can too.

Let us follow the apostle Paul's encouragement to pray without ceasing. Prayer is communion with God. This intimacy is not dependent on a place or an occasion. It is simply being with God. Whether in thanks or tears or in simply sharing our fears, prayer is powerful. Keep me praying, Lord. Amen.

Let your life be a prayer;
you can be sure God hears.

53

Giving Thanks

Give thanks in all circumstances; for this is
God's will for you in Christ Jesus.
1 THESSALONIANS 5:18 (NIV)

Thanksgiving is a celebration of God's goodness. We should give thanks in good and bad, difficult and easy circumstances. The apostle Paul reveals that it is God's will for us.

Today, let our attitude be one of gratitude to God for his goodness and his mercies. Let us give thanks and remember that God is with us, and he is for us. Let us use our lips to shout our thanksgivings. Thank you, Lord! Amen.

Giving thanks every day
is a wonderful way to pray.

54

Thinking Hard

Whatever is true, whatever is noble, whatever is right, whatever is pure, whatever is lovely, whatever is admirable—if anything is excellent or praiseworthy—think about such things.

PHILIPPIANS 4:8 (NIV)

It requires little effort to think negatively. Thoughts can barge in unannounced and without invitation. But we have the responsibility of sifting them out and determining whether they remain and how long they remain.

We are admonished to ponder thoughts that are positive and productive. Our thoughts should dwell on the positive, pure, and praiseworthy. Great Physician, we submit to open-mind surgery. Heal us, we pray. Amen.

Thinking about the positive
will displace the negative.

55

In Order

Guide my steps by your word, so I will not be overcome by evil.

PSALM 119:133 (NLT)

God's Word provides security and guidance for our footsteps. It establishes them and leads them along the right pathway.

Footsteps need this ordered pathway. Without order, feet tend to stray and eventually stumble. When we follow him, our feet remain firm and grounded. We pray, keep our feet, Lord. Amen.

When we call,
God guides our feet, lest we fall.

56

Are You Up?

Very early in the morning, while it was still dark, Jesus got up, left the house, and went off to a solitary place, where he prayed.

MARK 1:35 (NIV)

Mornings are generally fresh, filled with the dew of the past night and the promises of the new day. To access God's mercies, Jesus sought God's presence. His example is encouraging.

When you get up, go to a quiet place for a quiet time. Let the light of dawn shine on you there. You will get a good perspective, God's perspective. I am going, Lord. Amen.

Make no excuses.
Get up and go
to the place God chooses.

57

Show Off

For we are God's masterpiece. He has created us anew in Christ Jesus, so we can do the good things he planned for us long ago.

EPHESIANS 2:10 (NLT)

Pride and joy are emotions that artists experience when they see their work on display.

We are God's workmanship created to do God's work. When we do, God is pleased. He feels a sense of pride when we fulfill our purpose on earth. We become his prized trophies, and he shows us off. Ah, Lord God, help us to be worthy of your display. Amen.

We are God's masterpiece, God's prize.
Let's display the merchandise.

58

Peace Up

For he himself is our peace, who has made the two groups one and has destroyed the barrier, the dividing wall of hostility.

EPHESIANS 2:14 (NIV)

When things in our lives are broken and separated, peace is not possible, and the fulfillment of purpose is thwarted. Jesus was concerned about our brokenness, so he removed the barriers: religion, race, creed, class, and gender. He brought wholeness and peace.

Now nothing is broken. Everything is one whole. In Jesus, God has united us, bringing us into his fold. No more schisms, nothing to divide. Jesus, in you we have found a place to hide. Hallelujah! Amen.

Jesus, God's only Son,
removes barriers and makes us one.

59

Touching Faith

"Daughter, he said to her, your faith has made you well. Go in peace."
LUKE 8:48 (NLT)

Jesus spoke to a woman who was sick, penniless, and vulnerable. This woman had spent all she had and had nothing except a faith that was willing to touch Jesus. She reached out in her pain and plight and touched Jesus. She was made whole.

We, too, must touch God with faith. We have nothing else capable of reaching him. Lord, help us to touch you with the eyes, hands, and hearts of faith. Amen.

Faith to believe
is the window through which
we receive.

60

Love Gives

For God so loved the world, that he gave his only Son, that whoever believes in him should not perish but have eternal life.

JOHN 3:16 (ESV)

God is the greatest lover, and God is therefore the greatest giver. For God so loved that he gave.

Love knows only one thing, and that is how to give. Any authentic lover is a generous giver. Giving is the only demonstration of love. Whether patience, time, money, or any other resource, giving is a sign of love. If you love, then give. As you have given love, Lord, so we give. Amen.

What you are willing to give
is a telling indicator of how you live!

61

With Us

So the Word became human and made his home among us. He was full of unfailing love and faithfulness· And we have seen his glory, the glory of the Father's one and only Son.

JOHN 1:14 (NLT)

God entered the human arena by choice. He desired to be with us and to live among us as brothers. Jesus, who is the Word, became flesh; that is, he put on our humanity. He became like one of us so that we could become like him.

The truth is God gives us grace so that we can be loving just like him. This grace is greater than all our sin. There is hope for us. Thank you, Lord. Amen.

God broke through the barriers
of eternity just to keep our company.

62

Down to Raise Me Up

"I am the good shepherd. The good shepherd sacrifices his life for the sheep."

JOHN 10:11 (NLT)

This duty of the shepherd is to provide for and protect the sheep from every possible danger. A good shepherd would bravely face danger and risk his life to defend his sheep.

Jesus is that Good Shepherd who laid down his life for the sheep. Jesus makes the bold claim, "I am the Good Shepherd." He was forsaken so that we can be forgiven. He was rejected that we could be accepted. Thank you, Lord. Amen.

Jesus paid the ultimate sacrifice.
He put down his life to give us life.

63

Transfer Is Good

For he has rescued us from the dominion of darkness and brought us into the kingdom of the Son he loves.

COLOSSIANS 1:13 (NIV)

The domain of darkness is a dreadful, fearful place devoid of God's presence. God purchased with Jesus, the ticket that made our transfer possible.

We have been transferred from darkness to light, guilt to freedom, despair to hope, and death to life. The forces of darkness can no longer contain us, thanks to the blood of Jesus Christ. Thank you, Jesus. Amen.

A new position, new power,
new transfer this hour.

64

Look Up

Look up into the heavens. Who created all the stars?
He brings them out like an army, one after another,
calling each by its name. Because of his great power and
incomparable strength, not a single one is missing.

ISAIAH 40:26 (NLT)

God is aware of you and the circumstances that surround you. You are on his radar. He is watching you this minute. And yes, he knows your name. So, lift your eyes from your problem, from your circumstance. With God, nothing is left to chance.

Think about it. God created the stars with infinite wisdom and power, and as vast as the universe is, no star goes missing, not even for an hour. If he holds the stars, he can hold you. Thank you, Lord. Amen.

If you feel shaky, rest assured,
you are secured.

65

No Need to Fear

Fear not, for I am with you; be not dismayed, for I am your God; I will strengthen you, I will help you, I will uphold you with my righteous right hand.

ISAIAH 41:10 (ESV)

God is with us. He is our God. He gives the assurance of his help and comforting strength. He promises to support and to sustain. This promise we can count on.

Hear again the gracious promise of the Lord. "Do not be afraid, for I am with you. I am your God. I will strengthen you. I will help you." Where do you need help? God is standing near. Thank you for your promise and presence, Lord. Amen.

God's presence is his seal;
this guarantee is real.

66

Blessed People

Wherever you go and whatever you do, you will be blessed.
DEUTERONOMY 28:6 (NLT)

God has determined that we are a blessed people. He is the great blesser, the God who delights in blessing his children. God's blessings are expressions of his love and approval. This kind of blessing is not limited to but may include material possessions.

To be blessed is to be smeared, daubed up, and empowered for success. This special endowment enables us and makes all things possible. Whatever we do, wherever we go, we are blessed; we are covered with God's favor. Bless the Lord! Amen.

Remember you are blessed.
So let your heart rest.

67

New Strength

Don't be dejected and sad, for the joy of the Lord is your strength!
NEHEMIAH 8:10 (NLT)

Outward circumstances may affect my happiness, but they cannot touch my joy. God gives joy, and no one can take it away. With God's joy, I am strong and can face the challenges of life.

When the days are dark and the nights are long, when pain fills our hearts and there is no song, joy gives the strength to face the night and wait with hope for the morning light. Give me joy in my heart, Lord. Amen.

Let joy make you strong
and keep you when the night is long.

68

Together We Do It

"Let us start rebuilding." So they began this good work.

NEHEMIAH 2:18 (NIV)

Nehemiah knew the power of working together. He and the Jews had one mind and one purpose, and they accomplished the task of rebuilding Jerusalem's wall. They had a mind to work.

So much more can be accomplished when we work together. We can build anything. Nothing will be denied. Let us not be distracted by personalities but work together and accomplish endless possibilities. It is worth it. Accomplish your work in us, Lord. Amen.

Join hands with someone today.
Work together and pray.

69

Lost and Found

For the Son of Man came to seek and to save the lost.

LUKE 19:10 (NIV)

Without God, all of us are in a lost state. We would have remained there without the search and rescue effort of Jesus, who came with one mission, to seek and save souls that were lost.

It is impossible to be lost and not sustain some measure of bruising and wounding. The Lord Jesus seeks us out, and when he finds us, he offers us healing and hope. Thank you for looking for us and finding us, Lord. Amen.

I almost drowned.
Praise God, now I'm found.

70

New Eyes for Seeing

And what is the immeasurable greatness of his power toward us who believe, according to the working of his great might.

EPHESIANS 1:19 (ESV)

God's immeasurable power is working for us who believe. Every circumstance has to bow beneath God's power. And we have access to that power because we believe.

Our old eyes tend to see only the problem, but with new eyes, we see the solution. We are the solution because God is working through us to display his great might. Open our eyes, Lord, that we may manifest the hope to which you have called us. Amen.

New eyes are wise.
New eyes see otherwise.

71

When You Know

May have power, together with all the Lord's holy people, to grasp how wide and long and high and deep is the love of Christ, and to know this love that surpasses knowledge.

EPHESIANS 3:18–19 (NIV)

Knowledge is power, and the experience of knowing is powerful one. Experience, when it is proven, becomes truth, and truth tested over time becomes surety and confidence within.

When we know the love of Christ, we know that Christ's love is inexhaustible, unconquerable, and always available to us. We also know that because of God's love, we are destined for greatness. Greatness is God's love on the inside of us. God, help us to know your love. Amen.

This truth no one can disprove.
I know God's amazing love.

72

Treat Others Kindly

Be kind to one another, tender-hearted, forgiving one another, as God in Christ forgave you.
EPHESIANS 4:32 (ESV)

Kindness is the hallmark of great people. It manifests in forgiveness and caring concern for others. Kindness does not depend on kindness to be kind. It is in the presence of all that is unkind that kindness shines.

God first showed us this kindness when he forgave us. This deposit of God's kindness in us continues to multiply itself, and others benefit because it is there. We learn to forgive as we have been forgiven. Let me show kindness, Lord. Amen.

Let God's love fill your mind,
and remember to treat others kindly.

73

Melody Speaking

Singing psalms and hymns and spiritual songs among yourselves and making music to the Lord in your hearts.

EPHESIANS 5:19 (NLT)

Speech can sound rhythmical, but the melody is created when there is understanding, genuine sharing, mutual encouragement, and, of course, great singing.

We are encouraged to sing psalms, hymns, and spiritual songs. Our singing will encourage and lift others. Our singing also creates music in our hearts. This is a sure way of making a melody the Lord will enjoy. So, let us share the melody and sing a beautiful song. We love you, Lord. Amen.

True spirituality
is when God can hear in your heart
a melody.

74

Courage under God

Timothy, my dear son, be strong through the grace that God gives you in Christ Jesus.

2 TIMOTHY 2:1 (NLT)

Through Jesus, we have access to a certain enabling and empowering commodity called grace. This grace is given to us as a gift from God. We do not deserve it, but he gives it to us anyway.

This grace also makes it possible for us to face life. We live as overcomers because we are fortified with God's strength. Strength is therefore not the ability to master the other but the capacity to see we are nothing without the other. When we receive God's grace, we walk with courage under God. May we lean on you, O Lord. Amen.

Strength is our capacity
fortified with God's ability.

75

Power Spirit

For God gave us a spirit, not of fear but power and love and self-control.
2 TIMOTHY 1:7 (ESV)

We face giants in life regularly, and we often feel intimidated, powerless, and impotent, with little control. God has, however, given us the courage and power to defeat them and get the job done.

As kingdom people, we need to fulfill the mandate of God's kingdom. The mountains we meet may seem impossible to climb, and the rivers may appear too deep to cross. But we must be courageous, exercise discipline, and do the job. Help us, Lord. Amen.

The completion of your task,
God expects it.
Be disciplined and do it.

76

Safety Deposit Box

For I know whom I have believed, and I am convinced that he is able to guard until that Day what has been entrusted to me.

2 TIMOTHY 1:12 (ESV)

God has never lost a battle. Truly, he has already won the war. As people of God, we need to grow our faith in the one we believe is confident he will guard what he has given to us.

We can rest assured what we give to him, those things that are important to us, he will keep safe. He places them in his fireproof, time-proof, stormproof, and theft-proof box, for which he alone has the keys. We are safe with him. Live each day in victory. Thank you, Lord. Amen.

With God, we are well guarded
and warded.

77

Prophesy

So I spoke the message as he commanded me, and the breath came into their bodies. They all came to life and stood up on their feet—a great army.

EZEKIEL 37:10 (NLT)

We are always prophesying, whether under God's command or of our own volition. Let us be intentional and prophesy only as God commands.

When Ezekiel prophesied under God's command, he brought healing, hope, and life to his people. We, too, can be instruments of healing and hope to our people. As we prophesy, we must ensure that God is the one directing us. Then we will prophesy life rather than death and have victory in all we do. Help us, Lord. Amen.

No need to worry;
prophesy your way to victory.

78

He's Standing with You

But the Lord stood with me and gave me strength so that I might preach the Good News in its entirety for all the Gentiles to hear.

2 TIMOTHY 4:17 (NLT)

God is always willing to stand with you. When he gives you a task, he stands by you and gives you the strength to accomplish it.

This means you are never working by yourself. God is with you, strengthening you, increasing your capacity, and fulfilling his purpose in you. He is with you today. He is with you right now. He is strength like no other, and his strength reaches you. Thank you, Lord. Amen.

God's promise is true.
He is standing with you.

79

Holding a Watch

"I am the Lord; I have called you in righteousness;
I will take you by the hand and keep you."
ISAIAH 42:6 (ESV)

God is your fussy Father who watches over you, ensuring your safety. He holds your hand and gives you confidence for success. God is a keeping God who calls you to purpose, holds your hand, and walks with you into your destiny

You can therefore be confident and courageous as you journey through life. You will make it, for God is holding your hand and handling the things concerning your life. Praise the Lord! Amen!

God watches over you
and establishes your footsteps
under you.

80

Ask and Receive

He asked life of you; you gave it to him,
length of days forever and ever.
PSALM 21:4 (ESV)

God is a God who delights in giving his children their heart's desires. Whether peace, pardon, or prosperity, nothing is too great for God to give to us. What do you desire? Ask God, and he will give it to you.

The beautiful reality is God placed some of those desires in our hearts so we can give him the glory when he fulfills them. Let us acknowledge and express those desires to God and watch our awesome God fulfill them. We thank you, Lord. Amen.

My friends, let's ask and believe
from God's hands we will receive.

81

Singing All the Time

My heart, O God, is steadfast, my heart is steadfast; I will sing and make music.

PSALM 57:7 (NIV)

St. Augustine once said he who sings prays twice. Long after the prayer is ended, the song remains in the heart being offered to God as prayerful worship.

So, sing constantly, consistently, confidently, courageously, and continuously. When we sing, we fix our hearts and make them steadfast and firm. Tune our hearts, Lord, and fill them with songs. We will sing. Amen.

Let nothing take your song.
Sing all day long.

82

Unbreakable Bars

He strengthens the bars of your gates and blesses your people within you.

PSALM 147:13 (NIV)

Moments of weakness come to everyone and form part of our common human experience. In our weak moments, God gives us strength.

God reinforces and fortifies us in our weak places and makes us strong. God also assures us that everyone and everything associated with us will be protected. Even our future generations will be beneficiaries of his blessings. Yes, those yet unborn are covered too. Thank you, Lord! Amen.

God takes care of you.
Your children are blessed too.

83

Know Your Season

For everything, there is a season and a time
for every matter under heaven.
ECCLESIASTES 3:1 (ESV)

Human existence is predicated on time and the seasons of hatches, matches, and dispatches. Humans will always experience birth, marriage, death, and all that comes in between. Since this is the case, we need to know our times and seasons. Equally important is the necessity to use our time wisely.

Because life happens in seasons, there are seasons when things go well and there are seasons when they do not. There are seasons of growth and other seasons when everything is on the decline. In all seasons, help us to trust you, Lord! Amen.

Know your season.
Serve for the right reason.

84

What's Your Number Now?

Teach us to realize the brevity of life, so that we may grow in wisdom.

PSALM 90:12 (NLT)

Unlike God, who inhabits eternity, we exist in a realm of limited time. Since this is the case, we need to be wise and learn to number our days.

Numbering our days helps us to avoid procrastinating and time-wasting because it makes us see that we do not have forever; we only have now. Since our present moments and days will one day come to an end, it behooves us to spend them wisely. So, let us number our days and complete our purpose. Teach us to count, Lord. Amen.

Pay attention to your ways.
Be wise and number your days.

85

Stop Fretting

Do not fret because of those who are evil or be envious of those who do wrong.

PSALM 37:1 (NIV)

Do not worry or become anxious or overly concerned about people who practice evil. A preoccupation with them distracts you from your purpose.

Worrying and wanting to be like the wicked gets us nowhere. We need not waste time wondering about them. They will fade, and so will their influence. Pray for them. Lord, help us all to turn to you. Amen.

Worry less and pray more.
God has you covered for sure.

86

Birthing

My dear children, for whom I am again in the pains of childbirth until Christ is formed in you.

GALATIANS 4:19 (NIV)

Giving birth is a very labor-intensive process. It is hard work. However, the reward at the end of the process makes it worthwhile.

Leading others to Christ and disciplining them requires real effort. The result, however, is Christ is formed in them. What beautiful pain. Help us to labor, Lord. Amen.

Face the birth pains.
New life is forming again.

87

Change Is Coming

If someone dies, will they live again? All the days of my hard service. I will wait for my renewal to come.

JOB 14:14 (NIV)

God permits us to experience difficulties, trials, tribulations, and even death. God uses our trials to increase our faith. He promises restoration and renewal in the midst of them.

Job faced his difficult experiences with courage. He knew they could not outlast him. Job also knew that God would bring him through, so he determined to wait until his situation changed. The change we deserve and long for is coming. Let us wait for it to come. Help us to trust in periods of trials. Amen.

Let us wait in prayer.
Our change is near.

88

Go Beyond

And behold, the curtain of the temple was torn in two, from top to bottom.
MATTHEW 27:51 (ESV)

The temple curtain meant separation from the place where God's presence dwelt and the place where we could not go. Our sins and non consecration kept us out.

Jesus's death tore the curtain from top to bottom, giving us access. Now every hindrance has been removed. We can come to God uninhibited and unhindered. Let us go in boldly. Amen.

For certain,
now we can go beyond the curtain.

89

Avoid Entanglements

For freedom Christ has set us free; stand firm therefore, and do not submit again to a yoke of slavery.

GALATIANS 5:1 (ESV)

It is easy to become mixed up and mixed in with bad attitudes, habits, and lifestyles. This creates bondage. If this bondage of sin is not broken, it can lead to destruction and death.

Christ desires that we live as free people. He died to offer us this freedom. Let us fight to maintain this freedom and do all we can to ensure we stay free. Help us, Lord. Amen.

Christ has made you free.
So walk in victory!

90

Fruit Season

But the Holy Spirit produces this kind of fruit in our lives: love, joy, peace, patience, kindness, goodness, faithfulness, gentleness, and self-control.

GALATIANS 5:22–23 (NLT)

Fruit bearing is the mandate and purpose of every believer. Bearing fruit is evidence that the Holy Spirit is present. When he is present, it shows.

Each one of us must testify of the truth that the Spirit is present in our lives. When people see us, they look for evidence of the Spirit. He spreads his love, his joy, his peace, and so much more. Is he showing in your life? Let it be so. Amen.

When the Holy Spirit is in us,
he makes us fruitilicious!

91

Keep Doing

So let's not get tired of doing what is good. At just the right time we will reap a harvest of blessing if we don't give up.
GALATIANS 6:9 (NLT)

Doing good is hard work, especially if we are not appreciated and our good does not seem to make a difference. We may feel we are wasting time and nothing is happening. We may also be inclined to give up on doing good.

At these times, however, we must maintain our hope and focus. Let us focus on the big picture and not lose heart. Let us do good because it is good to do good. Help us keep doing good, Lord. Amen.

Good is watching.
The good we must keep doing.

92

You Can Only Give What You Have

"I have no silver and gold, but what I do have I give to you."
ACTS 3:6 (ESV)

We possess many things, but we often think that material things are what people need. We forget we have a smile; we have faith; we have joy. We have so much.

Peter and John did not have silver and gold; they only had Jesus and they were willing to give him to the lame man. They knew that if he received Jesus, he would have everything. Like them, we must be ready to give what we have. It may change someone's life. Increase our capacity to give, Lord. Amen.

Give to all, rich and poor.
Give and you will get more.

93

Bearing His Name

"Go, for Saul is my chosen instrument to take my message to the Gentiles and to kings, as well as to the people of Israel."

ACTS 9:15 (NLT)

God's chosen instruments are not always the ones we would choose readily. We would choose perfect, successful instruments that would yield a great benefit to us. God, however, chose weak ones. We are all unlikely candidates but for grace. God chose Saul, a murderer, a persecutor of his church, to be his witness.

Every day we live, we must bear Christ's name and sign to others. We must be living witnesses. We must be God's instrument and accomplish great exploits for him. May God help us live up to his choice of us. Help us, Lord. Amen.

Ambassador! Please represent.
You are a chosen instrument.

94

More Blessed

"It is more blessed to give than to receive."
ACTS 20:35 (NLT)

Giving has a great magnet attached to it; the more you give, the more you receive. We have been encouraged and blessed by the generosity of others. We can also affirm the pleasure we have derived from giving to others. The truth be told, we are more blessed when we give.

The blessings we receive therefore should never be hoarded but should be given freely, confident that the giving magnet will always ensure that we receive. Let us be a blessing to others, and our lives will become more blessed. Give us the desire to be more blessed, Lord. Amen.

God's generosity
equals your prosperity.

95

Peace Treaty

And he shall speak peace to the nations; his rule shall be from sea to sea; and from the river to the ends of the earth.

ZECHARIAH 9:10 (ESV)

Wherever God rules, there is peace. Peace is not the absence of turbulence but God's voice of power, speaking in the turbulence, saying, "Silence, stillness, wholeness, completeness, rest."

God's voice gives confidence and assurance. God's voice speaks to nations in turmoil, ravaged by war. God's voice is our balm and gives us calm. So, speak peace, Lord. My soul hears. Amen.

God's peace rules from sea to sea,
saying, "Peace to you, peace to me."

96

Surrounded

"And I will be to her a wall of fire all around, declares the Lord, and I will be the glory in her midst."
ZECHARIAH 2:5 (ESV)

God promises to be a wall of fire around his people. God's firewall keeps us safe and secure within. God's firewalls also protect us from the powers of darkness, and all the forces of hell are kept at bay.

When God's firewalls surround us, we are brilliant and as glorious as light shining on jewels. God's enemies see us reflecting his glory, and they acknowledge him as God. We are surrounded and protected. Send the fire down, Lord. Amen.

Fear not what comes your way.
Know God will protect you today.

97

He Knows His Own

The Lord is good, a strong refuge when trouble comes. He is close to those who trust in him.

NAHUM 1:7 (NLT)

When trouble comes, we need a place of shelter, a place where we can hide. God is this refuge—a safe stronghold in the day of trouble. We can trust in God, for he knows his own.

God knows the fine prints of your insurance policy with him. Whatever the claim, whatever the damage, whether fire or flood, your coverage is good with God. When you belong to him, you are never underinsured or uninsured. God is total reliance, without deductibles. Bless his name; he has you covered. Amen.

God is on his throne,
and he knows who are his own.

98

Look Out

"Look among the nations, and see; wonder and be astounded. For I am doing a work in your days that you would not believe if told."
HABAKKUK 1:5 (ESV)

God is doing a work in you this day. This work may not be visible to your human eyes, but God is working. Waiting on God may be disconcerting, even disorienting—just waiting and watching, hoping—but God is up to something.

God also invites us to pay attention to what he is doing. It will be wonderful. Your breakthrough may seem long in coming. Don't lose focus. Let your attention be fully riveted on God. Look out. He is coming. Give us patience, Lord, to keep looking out. Amen.

Look closely. Look intently.
God is working powerfully.

99

Be on Your Watch

I will climb up to my watchtower and stand at my guard post. There I will wait to see what the Lord says.

HABAKKUK 2:1 (NLT)

A guard post is a special place. It observes the coming and going of friend and foe. Guarding is both an offensive and defensive position. Guards needed to stay alert to hear and relay messages. They remained in their positions in case any messenger came.

Habakkuk knew the importance of remaining at his post. He remained there until he got word from the Lord. He waited for God's green light. Like him, let us keep standing at our post and watching for the Lord of Hosts. Help us so to be. Amen.

Pay attention and
wait for the Lord's instructions.

100

Make Up Your Mind

But Daniel resolved that he would not defile himself.

DANIEL 1:8 (ESV)

Daniel lived in captivity in the pagan Babylonian culture. He desired to serve God, although the pagan culture encouraged him to do otherwise. Daniel, however, made up his mind to honor God.

We, too, live in a secular culture, and like Daniel, we must be determined to honor God by not defiling ourselves. We will not achieve our goals halting between two opinions. Today we decide to be excellent and honor the Lord, God. Lord, we will serve you. Amen.

Lord, we will honor you
in all we say and do.

101

Seeing through the Darkness

He reveals deep and hidden things; he knows what is in the darkness, and the light dwells with him.

DANIEL 2:22 (ESV)

Some secrets are hidden from us, yet they are known to God. The past, the present, and the future lie open to God's complete knowing. This truth makes the difference. God is never caught off guard by the situations and circumstances of our lives because he knows all things.

God knows what is hidden in the dark and sees what is in the light. He will provide illumination and reveal them to us. Yes, God will see us through. Help us to trust you, Lord, in the dark or the light. Amen.

God knows all things,
so calm yourself and rest in him.

102

Power of the Word

But it is the Lord who did just as he planned. He has fulfilled the promises of the disaster he made long ago.

LAMENTATIONS 2:17 (NLT)

Many times, we make plans, but due to circumstances, lack of resources, and determined will, we are unable to accomplish them. When God proposes anything, he gets it done!

Long ago, God determined that he would save us. He accomplished this through Jesus's death on the cross. We have been redeemed. He completed a great transaction. One day, we will live and reign with him. Help us to be ready, Lord, Amen.

God commanded the word.
And the created order heard.

103

Pouring Out

Rise during the night and cry out. Pour out your hearts like water to the Lord.

LAMENTATIONS 2:19 (NLT)

Nights are generally known for being dark, and most of us use them for sleeping. When we sleep, we are exposed and vulnerable. At night, the struggles of the day come crushing in on us, and we tend to feel deep pain.

God, as a loving father, is moved by our pain and encourages us to use the nights to cry out to him. He is moved by the tears in our eyes and the cries of our hearts. When we pour out our hearts like water, he heals us. He rouses himself to action on our behalf, especially when we cry in the night watches. We are crying, Lord. Amen.

God hears our cries
when we cannot cope.
He heals our hurts and renews our hopes.

104

He Calls Your Name

"Fear not, for I have redeemed you; I have called you by name, you are mine."

ISAIAH 43:1 (ESV)

We are people of limited power, and often the circumstances of our lives are not under our control, we fear. The good news is God has purchased us and made us exclusively his. He has intimate knowledge of us, and he knows our names.

The God who knows us and owns us calls us by name. He tells us not to fear our unknown circumstances. There is no need to fear or crumble beneath the enemy's intimidation tactics. He is a defeated foe. Hear God calling your name. We thank you, Father and Redeemer. Amen.

Goodbye, fear!
My God redeems, and my God cares.

105

You're Coming Out

Behold, I am doing a new thing; now it springs forth … I will make a way in the wilderness and rivers in the desert.

ISAIAH 43:19 (ESV)

God is a God of newness and variety. He constantly causes new things to spring forth. Like an amazing gardener, he makes new things flourish.

Your life is a flower. The Lord planted you, and you are blooming. Perhaps it is difficult to see among the weeds that surround you, but God is working in you. Others will be drawn to him because of you. People will look at your life and be refreshed. Remember—as you grow, allow God's love to show. Thank you, Lord. Amen.

The way may wind, but look!
There is a path for you to find.

106

A Gentle Reminder

Put me in remembrance; let us argue together; set forth your case, that you may be proved right.
ISAIAH 43:26 (ESV)

Reminders are important. They help us to focus on a task, event, or, another important occurrence. God, too, needs reminders. God asks that we give him reminders. When we give him reminders about his Word, he fulfills them.

If you feel the need to, remind God of his promises to you. Remind him his Word is true. Remind him of all the times he came through. Remind him he has done what no man has done. Remind him he will do what no man can do. Hallelujah! Amen.

Give God a timely reminder.
The goods he will deliver.

107

My Rightful Share

"The Lord is my inheritance; therefore, I will hope in him!"
LAMENTATIONS 3:24 (NLT)

The Lord is your inheritance; he is yours for the keeps. This truth offers hope and peace and assures you of your just and rightful share.

The Lord is your portion, meaning the Lord is your all, and your all is the Lord's. It is a wonderful truth that enlarges and establishes you. This also means that available from God, the source, is your unlimited resource. Therefore, soul, be at rest in God and have hope. Hallelujah! Amen!

God is my source,
and God is my resource.

108

Never-Ending Love

The steadfast love of the Lord never ceases;
his mercies never come to an end; they are new
every morning; great is your faithfulness.
LAMENTATIONS 3:22–23 (ESV)

God's love is like an ocean. No matter how much water is removed, it remains at capacity. There is no end to God's love.

We make frequent withdrawals from God's love bank, yet it is never depleted. Every withdrawal is followed by an automatic renewal. God's love is always fresh, always new. God remains faithful to us, and God is always true. God, we celebrate you and what you can do. Thank you, Lord. Amen.

When God's steadfast love flows,
only peace my soul knows.

109

Prepare Your House

Zacchaeus, hurry and come down, for today. I must stay at your house.
LUKE 19:5 (NLT)

Today is the day! A day filled with opportunities, possibilities, power, and promises. Jesus interrupts the sameness of today with his offer of salvation.

Jesus is willing to enter the house of every sinner to give salvation. He entered Zacchaeus's house, and he is willing to enter yours. Like Zacchaeus, you need to hurry. Cease making excuses and open your house and heart to Jesus. He will come for tea. Come, Lord, Jesus. Amen.

Prepare your house for Jesus to stay.
Please hurry. He is on his way.

110

The Day Is Coming

I tell you, he will give justice to them speedily. Nevertheless, when the Son of Man comes, will he find faith on earth?
LUKE 18:8 (ESV)

Delays can be difficult to deal with. They are like blockages in a stream and stand in the way of our fulfilling our dreams. Delays place pressure on us and are inconvenient.

When we get frustrated because of the delays, we must understand this truth: delays are not denials. Take heart. Our God of justice is on his way. Come, Lord, come. Amen.

Don't be daunted
by God's seeming lack of speed;
your help is guaranteed.

111

First Things

Let me say first that I thank my God through Jesus Christ for all of you.
ROMANS 1:8 (NLT)

Thanksgiving should be the priority of our day and our lives. Our awareness of ourselves each day is a reason for thanksgiving and praise to God: God has blessed us with one more day.

Let's do first things first: God, we thank you through Jesus Christ. We thank you for your love and forgiveness, the gift of life, and the people you placed in our lives. Thank you for your healing and peace. Thank you for your prosperity and increase. Thank you, God, for everyone and everything. In Jesus's name. Amen.

Our Thanksgiving
is essential to daily living.

112

Forgiveness Canopy

"Blessed are those whose lawless deeds are forgiven, and whose sins are covered."
ROMANS 4:7 (ESV)

Sin is like a slave driver working us mercilessly without any possibility of gaining our liberty. Sin is putrefying, decaying, sickening. We need to cover it.

The best cover for sin is forgiveness. Iniquity prevents prosperity and fosters death and disability. Cover it. Lord, pardon our iniquity and cleanse our sin. Amen.

Forgiveness is God's canopy
for sin and iniquity.

113

Moving Out

Therefore, if anyone is in Christ, he is a new creation.
The old has passed away; behold, the new has come.
2 CORINTHIANS 5:17 (ESV)

No matter how familiar it is to you or how sentimental you feel about garbage, garbage belongs at the dump.

When God sorts old things, however, he does not discard but makes them over. He connects with the old and releases his power to make new. God can recover lasting beauty even from a garbage dump. God can extract from the dump a gold mine. What a God! Recover us, Lord. Amen.

At his leisure,
God takes our trash
and makes treasure.

114

Build for the Future

And I will bring my people Israel back from exile.
"They will rebuild the ruined cities and live in them."

AMOS 9:14 (NIV)

God is an excellent restorer. He delights in used parts and bruised people. He restores them and makes them beautiful and useful again.

He rebuilds what was broken and renews what was used. You are not to be discarded but dedicated for God's special use. Say, "Let me be beautiful for you, Lord. Amen."

God knows where you have been,
and he is rebuilding your every ruin.

115

Demonstrate Love

But God showed his great love for us by sending
Christ to die for us while we were still sinners.
ROMANS 5:8 (NLT)

People usually give love to those who show them love. If you love me, then I love you. But not so with God. He loved us when we were unlovable. He loved us when we were lawless and rebellious. When we spurned his love, he died for us.

Jesus's dying proved we are worthy of his love. His dying also transformed us from loveless to lovely. He made us lovable and capable of loving. Now we are worthy, and we are lovely. God be praised. Amen.

God's love is on demonstration.
Be grateful and show appreciation.

116

Seek and Live

This is what the Lord says to Israel: "Seek me and live."

AMOS 5:4 (NIV)

Living things have certain known characteristics; they eat, they breathe, they move. God gives an added dimension to life. To be filled with life, we must seek him.

To live, we must seek a steady supply of life-giving nutrients from God, the life-giving source. To seek God is to seek health, happiness, peace, and forgiveness. To seek God is to seek life itself. Let us seek God, for in God, life consists. Help us, Lord, to seek you with our whole hearts. Amen.

We live when God we seek.
We find his strength
when we are weak.

117

When Waters Roll

But let justice roll down like waters and righteousness like an ever-flowing stream.
AMOS 5:24 (ESV)

God is altogether just and altogether righteous. Justice and righteousness are his character traits. They are the foundation of his throne, and he ensures that we experience them. Everyone deserves justice.

Others have wronged us, and if we are truthful, we will admit that we have faltered too. We know for sure God will treat us with fairness. His justice and his righteousness flow to us. They are flowing right now. God will do right, and God expects us to do right. Help us, Lord. Amen.

When justice flows like water,
God's people are delivered.

118

Taken

But the Lord called me away from my flock and told me, "Go and prophesy to my people in Israel."

AMOS 7:15 (NLT)

In life, it is important to remember where God took you from. This prevents us from becoming comfortable in our present position, thinking this is where we have always been, missing where God is taking us.

We must recognize we are in process, and what we have become is God's doing. Remembering where the Lord took us from will keep us focused on where he is taking us. May God help us to follow. Amen.

Lord, help me to remember,
and I will go. I surrender.

119

Chosen

"For many are called, but few are chosen."

MATTHEW 22:14 (NLT)

God has been calling men and women since the dawn of creation. His call is simply, "follow me, work with me, partner with me." God called you too. Did you answer?

When you respond with a yes and say, "I'm available," God selects you, and you become chosen. My answer is yes, Lord. Amen.

You will be blessed
when you say, "Lord, yes!"

120

Here and Now

"The time is fulfilled, and the kingdom of God is at hand; repent and believe in the gospel."

MARK 1:15 (ESV)

Now is a special time to hear the declaration of God's imminent kingdom. Repent and believe the gospel! Yes, now is the best moment to believe that Jesus loves you and died to save you, and now he offers you life abundantly. What is your response?

I trust you can recognize God's presence. He is life's essence, and he is near you right now. Now then is the opportune moment. It is the only moment you are sure of. It may even be the last one. I receive you and bow now, Lord. Amen.

Use your now moment fast
because now won't last.

121

Come Away

"Come away by yourselves to a desolate place and rest awhile."
MARK 6:31 (ESV)

We live fast-paced lives in a fast-paced world. We are therefore challenged to find rest. Jesus gave his disciples the invitation to come and rest awhile.

Rest comes only when we leave the entanglements and encumbrances behind and go with Jesus. Come to Jesus—to peace, hope, and provision. Come to his presence. Giving true rest is Jesus's style, and you find it when you sit with him for a while. Help us to rest, Lord. Amen.

Come away and find rest today!
Let Jesus be your hope, your joy, your stay.

122

Keep It In

"It is what comes from inside that defiles you."
MARK 7:20 (NLT)

Jesus says that what comes out of us defiles us. It follows then that there are defiling agents on the inside. Jesus's words challenge us to do an inventory of the inside to locate the contaminants.

If we do, we are likely to discover sin within. When we do, we need to put sin in quarantine and apply the disinfecting power of Jesus's blood. Let us ask the Lord to cleanse and cover our mouths. It is the only thing that will stop sin from proceeding out. Amen.

There is no doubt
we can stop sin from proceeding out.

123

I'm Listening

"Speak, Lord, your servant is listening."
1 SAMUEL 3:9 (NLT)

God speaks to us all the time, but quite often we are not prepared to listen. Consequently, we do not hear.

To hear God speak, we need to do several things. We need to quiet ourselves and engage in listening. So cease from your busying and speaking and start listening. Lord, give us ears to hear. Amen.

Shh! Are you listening?
God is speaking.

124

What Do You Have?

But with you, there is forgiveness, that you may be feared.

PSALM 130:4 (ESV)

Many people struggle with forgiveness. We find it difficult to forgive those people who have done us wrong. God, however, is generous with forgiveness.

God's forgiveness is an expression of his love. It quickens us to respect and revere his name. We come to a place of reverence and fear not because God is powerful but because God is merciful. Lord, we stand in awe of your love. Teach our hearts to fear you, Lord. Amen.

Forgiveness is not our achievement
but God's great investment.

125

Use It for Something

As God's co-workers, we urge you not to receive God's grace in vain.
2 CORINTHIANS 6:1 (NIV)

God gave us his grace to empower us for success. His grace provides all that we need to live godly in this world. There is a real temptation, however, to become familiar with it, squander it, and misuse it.

Let us not abuse God's grace but rather use it wisely—use it for the purpose God intended. Let us fulfill our life's purpose and live in his embrace. Grant our desire, Lord. Amen.

Don't waste God's grace.
Use it to seek God's face.

126

As Promised

"And now, Lord God, keep forever the promise you have made concerning your servant and his house. Do as you promised."

2 SAMUEL 7:25 (NIV)

David asked God to fulfill his promised word spoken to him. He was sure that God's word was the one thing he could depend on in life. He could trust God's word.

God is mindful of his word. He watches over it to perform and fulfill it. He does as he has promised. You, too, must remember your word is your bond and pledge. It establishes your character. It is important to fulfill it every time. Lord, help us to keep our word. Amen.

The best promise ever heard,
God always delivers on his word.

127

Don't Forget

Be careful not to forget the Lord, who rescued you from slavery in the land of Egypt.
DEUTERONOMY 6:12 (NLT)

I don't believe it is possible to forget God. I have discovered, however, that we can become so sufficient in ourselves and our achievements that we forget we need God.

Self-satisfaction can lead to complacency, which in turn can lead to lapsed attention, poor choices, and finally forgetting our need for the God who brought us thus far. We must therefore heed God's Word. Be aware of the tendency to forget and avoid regret. Lord, help us to remember! Amen.

Be careful to heed God's Word
and not to forget the Lord.

128

The Way to Pray

Pray then like this: "Our Father in heaven, hallowed be your name. Your kingdom come, your will be done, on earth as it is in heaven. Give us this day our daily bread."

MATTHEW 6:9–11 (ESV)

Prayer is being with God. It is simply basking in his presence, allowing his love to fill us, and expressing our love to him.

When we pray in this way, we hallow God's name and acknowledge our dependency on God's generosity. God provides, and we know he takes his responsibility seriously. When we ask, he gives us bread. He gives us all we need. Thank you, Lord. Amen.

The Our Father is a simple way
we can pray.

129

Turn Around

Our God turned the curse into a blessing.

NEHEMIAH 13:2 (NLT)

Sometimes in life, we experience challenges that burden us and knock us to the ground—when the forces of darkness surround all our paths, and we are convinced we are going down. But we give it to God, and he turns it around. Yes, God turned the curse into a blessing.

God can do anything. God can even turn the curse into a blessing. Then the trial becomes a triumph, and the test a testimony. Be sure God has a use for what seems like a curse in your life. Look. He's made it a blessing. Thank you, Lord.

Friends, let us make a joyful sound.
Our God turned the curse around.

130

For Real

"Behold, the fear of the Lord, that is wisdom, and to turn away from evil is understanding."

JOB 28:28 (ESV)

Fear of the Lord is a holy and healthy respect for God. It is not trepidation but reverence. We fear God because he is the Sovereign Lord of the land and sea. He was and is and will always be. To fear God is to be wise. When we fear God, we realize that he keeps us alive because we are special in God's eyes.

Because we love and respect him, we make a deliberate turn from what is evil and from what displeases him. This is the evidence of our godly fear. It also indicates that wisdom is near. Lord, teach us to fear you. Amen.

Holy, godly fear
is evidence that wisdom is near.

131

Peace in Christ

Peace be with all of you who are in Christ.
1 PETER 5:14 (NLT)

Christ himself is our peace. He is the one who holds all the broken pieces of our lives together. When the pieces come together, there is wholeness. Then follows peace, pardon, prosperity, and increase.

Christ the peacemaker gives his peace to all who are in him. Christ heals divisions; lifts burdens; frees us from prisons; and guides us to make the right decisions. He brings complete wholeness, and that is peace. In Christ, there is peace and more peace. Thank you for peace, Lord. Amen.

In Christ, we have perfect and
profound peace.
In Christ, all our struggles cease.

132

The Same-Minded God

For the gifts and the calling of God are irrevocable.
ROMANS 11:29 (ESV)

God's calling is never without his gift giving and blessing. God gives gifts to whoever he calls. It is his gift giving that enables our serving. He equips us for service extraordinaire.

God does not repossess or recall his gifts and graces for desertion and dereliction of duty. Instead, he gives us other opportunities to serve. God has called, equipped, and endowed you for his service. Heed the call and serve one and all. Help us, Lord. Amen.

Strengthen your arm and nerve.
God still expects you to serve.

133

Aim to Please

So we make it our goal to please him, whether we are at home in the body or away from it.

2 CORINTHIANS 5:9 (NIV)

Approval from others is important. It provides affirmation and builds confidence. Receiving approval from others should not be our aim but honoring God and blessing his name. God's approval brings his smile, which lasts an incredibly long while.

God's approval brings his blessings, releasing to us God's everything. I think we should make it our business then to please the Lord. Lord, we ask not for money or fame. May our desire to please you be our aim. Help us, Lord. Amen.

Our desire is not for money or fame
but to please your name.

134

What Do You Keep before You?

I keep my eyes always on the Lord.

PSALM 16:8 (NIV)

There are many benefits to be experienced if we keep the Lord before us. We will never be led astray because the Lord will guide our way. We will have all that we need because God will intercede. We will fulfill our destiny, and we will walk in victory. What more do we need?

Let us not be distracted but keep our eyes on the Lord. Let us focus on God and what he has done in our lives. Yes, let's keep him before our eyes. He will hear us when we pray and provide the strength to face each day. Lord,we set you before us today. Amen.

When we keep the Lord before,
we are blessed forevermore.

135

When Love Rejoices

It does not rejoice at wrongdoing but rejoices with the truth.
1 CORINTHIANS 13:6 (ESV)

Love is powerful, strong, and resilient. It bears, it believes, it hopes, and, yes, it rejoices. Love is deliberate and selective about its times of rejoicing. Love does not rejoice when ugly or evil is near but rejoices when the truth is celebrated.

Love holds truth and righteousness as companions dear. When love keeps company with truth, the kingdom of heaven comes near. The question is, With whom are you keeping company? Can love rejoice because of your choice? Lord, enable us to give love reason to rejoice. Amen.

Give love a reason to rejoice.
Truth is a good choice.

136

Kept

What's more, I am with you, and I will protect you wherever you go.

GENESIS 28:15 (NLT)

It is so relieving to know that I do not have to come up with the wisdom to keep myself. God is present with me, and he does the keeping.

God keeps me on the mountain. He keeps me in the valley. He keeps me when I'm happy, and he keeps me when I'm sad. He keeps me when I've been obedient, and he keeps me even when I'm rebellious and bad. God is with me constantly and protects me completely. Hallelujah! Amen.

You have no reason to fret;
you are wondrously kept.

137

Just Go

Therefore go and make disciples of all nations.
MATTHEW 28:19 (NIV)

Jesus commands us to go and disciple nations and peoples. This great task can only be accomplished by people with great obedience and total dependence on a great God.

Jesus gave us instructions to go and make followers. What qualifies us to go? God's choice of us does. We must live by example, showing dependability and integrity. We should demonstrate initiative and a willingness to serve others, leaving a footprint for others to follow. Show us how to lead, Lord. Amen.

Go and make disciples! Lead!
Live by your God-given creed.

138

Surrounded

Therefore, since we are surrounded by such a great cloud of witnesses … let us run with perseverance the race marked out for us.
HEBREWS 12:1 (NIV)

Running a race requires effort, energy, and enthusiasm. Running to win the race demands diligence, discipline, and determination. Sometimes runners get tired, but their focus on the finish line gives them the power to complete.

When we get tired in life's race, let's look to the finish line. There we will see Jesus waiting. On the sides are the witnesses who have completed the race. They are cheering us to victory. Come on. You are almost home. Thank you, Lord. Amen.

Lord, I am running the race.
I am a winner by your grace.

139

Custom-Made

You made all the delicate, inner parts of my body
and knit me together in my mother's womb.
PSALM 139:13 (NLT)

God is personally acquainted with your delicate parts. Each has been specially crafted from a unique mold. Friend, you are an original creation, the only one of your kind. God handcrafted you with great care. He designed your personality, your looks, even your hair. In your mother's womb, he stamped you an original.

It will take you an eternity to discover all that you are. So don't waste time imitating others. Do not live as a counterfeit. Be the original masterpiece that you are. Help us, Lord. Amen.

You were crafted with great care.
You are unique, precious, and rare.

140

I Love My Neighbor

"Do not seek revenge or bear a grudge against a fellow Israelite, but love your neighbour as yourself."

LEVITICUS 19:18 (NLT)

In our fallen world, we get hurt by others and often bear a grudge. When we judge the offender, we don't allow God to be the just judge. We also deny ourselves a fair hearing, compromise our justice, and lose the opportunity to love.

Rather than judging, let us be loving. Replace the demand for justice with a willingness to show grace. When we love our neighbor, we love ourselves. Lord, help us not to bear a grudge, but give us the capacity to love. Amen.

Listen up. Do yourself a favor:
love yourself by loving your neighbor.

141

Knowing and Doing

Teach me, O Lord, the way of your statutes;
and I will keep it to the end·

PSALM 119:33 (ESV)

Embedded deep within us is the consciousness of right and wrong and the desire to do the right. When faced with challenging circumstances that evoke deep emotions, however, we often do the opposite. This proves that knowing does not always produce doing.

We have been taught God's statutes by God and his appointed ambassadors. Now, like the psalmist, let us ask God for the enabling grace to keep them to the end, especially when it is difficult. Lord, give us the courage and commitment to follow you all the way. Give us the courage, Lord. Amen.

Follow the right
and lead others to the light.

142

Who Do You Call Friends?

No longer do I call you servants … but
I have called you friends.
JOHN 15:15 (ESV)

Trustworthiness, reliability, helpfulness, faithfulness, supportiveness, and loyalty are some of the required characteristics in a good servant or treasured in a good friend. God sees me as all this and more. He no longer calls me a servant but his friend.

Wow! This is a definite privilege and a tremendous honor. What an awesome vote of confidence God has in me. Lord, Jesus, you believe in me more than I believe in myself. You trust me more than I do myself. Lord, help me to live up to your expectations and be a true friend to the end. Amen.

Friends forever—
nothing our relationship can sever.

143

God Honors My Preference

He makes me lie down in green pastures,
he leads me beside quiet waters.
PSALM 23:2 (NIV)

God knows my history. He knows when I nearly drowned and why. He knows why gurgling waters intimidate me. Yet he does not make fun of me or my weaknesses. He is not humored by my distress.

The Lord acknowledges me where I am with fears and insecurities and leads me to a place where I am comfortable and comforted. Thank you, Lord. Amen.

God leads beside waters that are still.
There I abide and rest in his will.

144

Today

Jesus answered him, "Truly I tell you, today you will be with me in Paradise."

LUKE 23:43 (NIV)

Paradise with God is the guarantee authenticated by Jesus the Christ. This guarantee is not based on human goodness; we have none to give. It is not based on human strength; we are weak. This guarantee was offered because of one man's repentance and sealed by Jesus's love.

Christ desires for us to be with him in paradise. He opens paradise to us when we repent and turn to him. Lord, to you we turn our eyes. Thank you for opening paradise. Amen.

God, who is all-powerful and wise,
opens to us his paradise!

145

Do Hear

But don't just listen to God's word. You must do what it says. Otherwise, you are only fooling yourselves.

JAMES 1:22 (NLT)

Some people are willing to listen to God's Word but are not willing to obey it. The truth is hearing is easy, but obeying is not easy to do. Doing suggests we have internalized what we have heard.

The evidence of true hearing is doing. It is only when we obey and do that we prove we have heard. To hear and not to do is to fool ourselves. In doing, we receive the full benefit of our hearing. Lord, help us to hear and do. Amen.

Let God's Word get into you.
Then you will both hear and do.

146

What's Your Mindset?

Think about the things of heaven, not the things of earth.
COLOSSIANS 3:2 (NLT)

The things of earth are right before us, tempting, teasing, testing, and telling us life is not life without them. It is easy to set our minds on the things of earth. After all, we can see, smell, taste, touch, and handle such things. Things of the earth are, however, only temporal and do not prepare us for eternity.

We need a new mindset, one focused on heaven. This is necessary if abundant life is to be part of our experience. We need to let go of the earthly to embrace the heavenly. We dare not hold earth and lose heaven. Help us, Lord. Amen.

As recipients of God's love,
let us set our minds on things above.

147

Service without Complaint

Show hospitality to one another without grumbling.

1 PETER 4:9 (ESV)

Hospitality is a special grace that makes people feel welcomed and at home. Service is easy if the people you serve are appreciative and courteous but challenging if the people being served are ungrateful.

We must be hospitable to all. We must resist the temptation to be vindictive or aggressive and diminish the quality of the service to those who are ungrateful. Do not complain but remember we are serving God through them. Lord, help us serve with excellence. Amen.

You serve in heavenly style
when you serve with a smile.

148

Before the Foundations

Even before he made the world, God loved us and chose us in Christ to be holy and without fault in his eyes.

EPHESIANS 1:4 (NLT)

You are not an afterthought. Long before the foundations of the world were established, you were planted in the heart of God. God loves you and chose you in Christ so that you could live holy and without fault.

This means that you and all that concerns you are important to God. Before God made the foundations, God put you in his heart. God chose you to live set apart. This is so incredibly awesome! Thank you, Lord. Amen.

Remember God loved you from the start
and placed you in his heart.

149

Trouble Can't Last

For our light and momentary troubles are achieving for us an eternal glory that far outweighs them all.

2 CORINTHIANS 4:17 (NIV)

We live in a fallen world in which we see destruction, darkness, and death. This means that troubles in life are common and affect everyone.

It is important to remember that troubles come to punish you so you can reflect God's glory. So, in troublesome times, learn to relax your mind and remember troubles are only trying to bring out of you a glorious shine. Help us to shine for you. Amen.

Troubles, too, shall pass;
yes, they certainly cannot last.

150

Detected Right Through

My frame was not hidden from you when I was made in the secret place when I was woven together in the depths of the earth.

PSALM 139:15 (NIV)

The ultrasound is not a new invention or a modern phenomenon. God has been taking ultrasounds from forever. God took one while you were being fashioned in your mother's womb. He saw you there unformed. He handled your delicate parts and wove them together in an intricate way.

God is aware of you. He made you perfect. He ensured there was no mistake, no fault. You did not escape his radar. He knows where and how you are right now. You are so precious. Awesome God, thank you. Amen.

God is with you.
He still takes care of you.

151

Good Suffering

Indeed, all who desire to live a godly life in Christ Jesus will be persecuted.

2 TIMOTHY 3:12 (ESV)

Suffering and its attendant pain can be quite difficult to bear. I believe if we had a choice, we would ensure that suffering was not part of our human experience. The reality is, if we seek to live right in Christ, we will experience persecution.

We feel the pain of persecution more when we suffer unjustly, when we are accused wrongfully, and when we are disgraced shamefully. When we suffer for Christ, however, it is good suffering because it is God-suffering. Help us, Lord, when we experience suffering for you to know that it is good suffering. We need grace, Lord. Amen.

Make sure your suffering is God-suffering.
Then it will be good suffering.

152

Walk Well

So as to walk in a manner worthy of the Lord, fully pleasing to him, bearing fruit in every good work and increasing in the knowledge of God.

COLOSSIANS 1:10 (ESV)

God is interested in the way we live our lives. He is interested in how we walk, and he encourages us to walk in a way that pleases him. When our steps are ordered by God's divine mandate and empowered by the Holy Spirit, God is fully pleased. Our lives are fruitful, our knowledge of God increase, and God receives glory.

When we walk worthy of the Lord, we are living witnesses of our faith. Walking worthy requires concentrated, continuous, committed effort. There is no time to look away or look around. There is just enough time to follow in God's steps. Lord, may our walk please you. Amen.

When the Holy Spirit with us dwell
We will walk well.

153

Shine Your Light

In the same way, let your good deeds shine out for all to see so that everyone will praise your heavenly Father.

MATTHEW 5:16 (NLT)

Light is essential to life. It provides the source of energy that sustains life forms in the universe. Yet many people still stumble in the dark. They need the light of Jesus to see life's path and discover their purpose.

We who know Christ need to live our lives so others can see him shining in us. His light will dispel the darkness of their situations and give them hope. They need us to light the path for them to follow. When we illuminate their path, they will praise the Lord. Give us the strength to shine, Lord. Amen.

Remember to shine.
Shine all the time.

154

Pleasant Things

How wonderful and pleasant it is when brothers live together in harmony!

PSALM 133:1 (NLT)

Unity is the willingness to make space for the other. It involves making personal adjustments that bring you to a place of oneness with the other person while allowing the other to be. No wonder unity is pleasant.

God dwells in complete unity, Father, Son, and Holy Spirit. They are separate but not separated. They are different but not divided. God has endowed us with the same Godhead capacity. He gives us the ability to dwell together in harmony. Unity is love in action. Help us, Lord. Amen.

Make some personal space.
Walk with another by God's grace.

155

Safe House

The name of the Lord is a strong tower; the righteous man runs into it and is safe.

PROVERBS 18:10 (ESV)

In the world of many threats, we need a safe house, a place to run and hide. May I invite you to consider the name of the Lord as your safe house?

The name of the Lord is powerful. It is a place where you can run and hide. It is a shelter, a shade from the heat, a stronghold in the day of trouble, and it serves as a safe retreat. Trust in the name of the Lord. It will keep you safe. Thank you, Lord. Amen.

God is a safe house in which to hide.
God will protect you on all sides.

156

Always Available

Evening, morning, and noon I cry out in distress and he hears my voice.

PSALM 55:17 (NIV)

A visit to the doctor necessitates an appointment that may have to be made months in advance because the physician is booked up. It is comforting to know that God's calendar can always accommodate us. He hears our voice.

God is never too busy and never overbooked but is always available to us, whether morning, noon, or evening. Whatever time we call, God hears. We are never in the waiting line, because our God is always available. Bless our God! Amen.

God is available my cries to hear.
God is available; he is always near.

157

Hide It

I have hidden your word in my heart that
I might not sin against you.
PSALM 119:11 (NIV)

God's Word is of supreme value. It is a powerful force lighting our path and directing our way. We must take the time to study, then hide its truth in our hearts.

When we treasure God's Word in our hearts, its power is released in us and prevents us from sinning. The power of God's Word strengthens us to overcome the power of temptation. God's Word will keep us from sin's power, every hour. Help us, Lord. Amen.

God's Word gives light
and will direct us aright.

158

Just Because

But God, being rich in mercy, because of his great love … even when we were dead in our trespasses, made us alive together with Christ.

EPHESIANS 2:4–5 (ESV)

You stood no chance of selection. You simply did not qualify. But because of the kindness of God's heart, God loved you and chose, 'and gave you a 'bly'

God selected you and made you a part of the family of Christ. You had no credentials, no collateral to offer, but God chose you. God is generous with his mercy. He forgave your sin and allowed you to qualify and come in. Now you are no longer dead but alive through Christ's mercy! Thank you. Amen.

God loves you; it is true.
He shows mercy in all you do.

159

Loving and Lifting

Bear one another burdens, and so fulfill the law of Christ.

GALATIANS 6:2 (ESV)

Life is not exempt from burdens. We all carry our share. Even though we have our own, it is important to let others know we care. So our brothers' and sisters' burdens we must learn to bear.

Bearing means holding up, supporting, or being the one others can stand on. Someone is counting on you to be there for them. So share your strength. You will become stronger when you do, when you lift others too. Show us how to bear, Lord. Amen.

We show we care
when others' burdens we bear.

160

Due Season Coming

So let's not get tired of doing what is good. At just the right time we will reap a harvest of blessing if we don't give up.
GALATIANS 6:9 (NLT)

We do good not because it is expected of us but because it is good to do good. Doing good also pays dividends that require a due season, which is a time of waiting. Many people lose heart during this waiting period; they give up and miss their blessing

Let us not get tired and ready to give up. Keep sowing. Keep the faith! The time for sowing will soon end. Then you will reap your harvest of blessing. Give strength to sow, Lord. Amen.

God is a God of seasons.
Celebrate. That's a good reason.

161

Tomorrow's Worry Canceled

Therefore do not worry about tomorrow, for tomorrow will worry about itself. Each day has enough trouble of its own.

MATTHEW 6:34 (NIV)

When challenging situations occur, it is easy to worry and fret. Worry is a preoccupation with self and its outcomes. It happens when we trust in our ability rather than in God to take care of our needs. It takes discipline not to worry.

Jesus encourages us to focus on today and not worry about tomorrow. He cancels tomorrow's worry by making us aware that tomorrow will take care of tomorrow. If we worry about tomorrow, we will fail to enjoy today. On you, Lord, we cast tomorrow's cares, and we trust you with today. Amen.

You only have today.
Don't worry and waste it away.

162

I Am Still Thirsty

As the deer longs for streams of water,
so I long for you, O God.
PSALM 42:1 (NLT)

God is the source of life. He is water to the thirsty, bread to the hungry, strength to the weary, and hope for the dreary. My soul desires for you to fill me.

I acknowledge, Lord, that there is an emptiness within me that I tried to fill with knowledge, business, fame, status, and everything I could lay hold of. The emptiness is still there. I am still thirsty. So, Lord, I turn to you. Fill me with yourself. Amen.

Lord, fill my empty cup.
It is all turned up.

163

Exceeding Grace

The grace of our Lord was poured out on me abundantly, along with the faith and love that are in Christ Jesus.

1 TIMOTHY 1:14 (NIV)

Grace is God's goodness and mercy reaching out to us. The truth is God's grace is always extended toward us. When grace is exceedingly abundant, it pursues us beyond the turns and meanders of our lives. So do its companions, faith and love.

Grace touches us wherever we are, wherever we hurt, wherever we have need. It is touching us now. So let us live our lives and drown ourselves in the sea of God's grace. We are sinking, Lord, for all your grace that's available to us. Bless you, Lord! Amen.

Celebrate God's grace.
In every kindness, his hand we trace.

164

Poor Yet Rich

God blesses those who are poor.

MATTHEW 5:3 (NLT)

When God blesses the poor, he empowers them for success and enables them to be a blessing. Being poor is not a condition of one's estate but the character and attitude of one's heart. When God blesses me, I am empowered for success, and greatness lies inside me.

To be blessed by God means that despite the limitations of my sphere, there is hope, joy, and success. I recognize that God is my source and I am a transshipment point. To be blessed means that I am a force that cannot be contained. No wonder the kingdom of heaven belongs to me. Keep us poor in spirit, Lord. Amen.

When in spirit I am poor,
I am blessed all the more.

165

The Need to Pray

I urge, then, first of all, that petitions, prayers, intercessions, and thanksgiving be made for all people—for kings and all those in authority.

1 TIMOTHY 2:1–2 (NIV)

It is very commonplace for us to criticize and curse governments and people in authority. We observe their abuses and misuses. We hear their excuses for their excesses. The truth is they need help. We help them when we pray for them.

What should we pray? We should pray that justice and equality be the hallmark of their leadership. Pray that they acknowledge the Lord as Savior and allow his light to lead and direct their path. Pray that we lead a godly life under them. Let's pray to God to bless our government. Amen.

We pray that God's light
leads leaders to do right.

166

Hand Help

Give me a helping hand, for I have chosen to follow your commandments.

PSALM 119:173 (NLT)

God is delighted when we keep his precepts. He offers us his hand of help so we can be successful. God's right hand is full of power and might. He employs that power on our behalf when we choose to keep his commands.

Amid life's challenges, we can be confident of God's helping hand. We can count on God to keep his promise to help us in times of need. Yes, God keeps his without fail. We ask for your helping hand, God, for we are willing to obey your command. Thank you, Lord. Amen.

The Lord's strong arm
saves his people from all harm.

167

Fresh Look

But when you fast, comb your hair and wash your face.
MATTHEW 6:17 (NLT)

Fasting is a decision to humble oneself before God. It is to prostrate one's heart before God's feet. Fasting is a change in our heart's position and our indication to God we are ready to follow his instruction.

Our fasting should be accompanied by the display of a cheerful countenance. Our humility is not to be demonstrated by the outward piety of a long face but the hidden purity of God's grace. A brightened face expresses our delight to obey. So, with anointed head, we seek God's face. Thank you, Father. Amen.

Fasting provides grace,
giving us the opportunity,
God's blessings to taste.

168

Sure Healing

Jesus said to him, "Shall I come and heal him?"
MATTHEW 8:7 (NIV)

Jesus is committed to our healing. He is a healer, doctor, and restorer. We note that Jesus the healer is willing to come to where we are to meet our needs. Yes, he takes the initiative to come to us.

We note as well that Jesus is never daunted by the nature of the degree of our disease. He knows them all and cures them all. Every disease melts into nothing under the healing power of his blood. Whatever the disease you have, Jesus offers you a cure. Rest assured he will come and heal you. Yes, he will. Thank you, Lord. Amen.

God has the strategy
to heal all our maladies.

169

Speech Matters

But I tell you that everyone will have to give account on the day of judgment for every empty word they have spoken.

MATTHEW 12:36 (NIV)

Words are powerful and possess unique characteristics. They never dissipate, never disappear, and never die. Words somehow can remain forever. It does not matter who speaks them; words must be accounted for.

Jesus warned us that we have to give an account for careless words uttered without regard or concern for others or the advancement of his kingdom. Let us be careful and ponder with diligence the words we speak, for the words themselves will hold us accountable. Help us to be careful, Lord. Amen.

It might be a bore and a drudge,
but watch your words, lest they carry you before the judge.

170

No Fear

Have no fear of them, nor be troubled.

1 PETER 3:14 (ESV)

What or who do you fear? People and situations may cause us to fear. As long as we are in the world, we will face them, yet we are encouraged not to be fearful because of them. How is this possible?

This is possible because we need not surrender to outside forces that cannot destroy us if we have surrendered to the Inner Force who can preserve and prosper us. We trust you, Lord, and choose not to fear. Amen.

God is near.
I will never be troubled.
I will never fear!

171

Two Different Looks

Man looks on the outward appearance,
but the Lord sees the heart.
1 SAMUEL 16:7 (ESV)

Human beings have natural eyes, so we see naturally. We see what we feel, think, and hear. We see only by sensing. God, however, goes beyond the natural and sees what he knows. God knows the heart, thoughts, and intentions of the heart; therefore, he looks at the heart.

God is the heart's programmer and knows the heart's circuitry. God sees the heart's electrical impulses. When we are on the outside looking in, he is already on the inside looking out. He alone is blessed with such an unlimited vision, so we pray, heal our hearts, Lord. Amen.

God knows how
the heart's circuitry flows.
He goes by what he knows.

172

Who Are We Really?

What is mankind that you are mindful of them,
human beings that you care for them?
PSALM 8:4 (NIV)

Human beings are the most celebrated of God's created order. We are made in the likeness of God, and we are mandated to walk in dominion. God is the loving creator who desires to manifest his glory through us human beings.

What is humankind? We are the crown, the joy, and the delight of God's creation. God thinks about us because when God sees us, God sees himself. He sees the hope that we can be like him. This is marvelous. We are lost in wonder, love, and praise! Amen.

God made us worthy.
Let us manifest God's glory.

173

Two Edges

"Come, let us return to the Lord. He has torn us to pieces; now he will heal us."
HOSEA 6:1 (NLT)

When bones are not set right, the surgeon breaks them to put them right. In this act, we see love can inflict wounds to bring healing.

When we walk away from God, we become torn and wounded and need healing. God chastises us to restore us in righteousness. His hand hurts, but his hand also heals. In our sinful wonderings, we may have been wounded by God, but in our returning to him, we will be healed. So what are you waiting for? Come let us return. Heal us, Lord. Amen.

Turning from God causes pain!
Returning to God brings healing rain!

174

Funny Words

The words you say will either acquit you or condemn you.

MATTHEW 12:37 (NLT)

Our words are powerful and tricky. They can free us or put us in prison. They support us when spoken in truth and strip us bare when spoken in error.

It is important to know the intention of our words before we embrace them with our lips. Let us employ the diligence and patience to examine our words while they are still in our mouths. By so doing, we ensure that they never have the power to condemn us. Remind us, Lord. Amen.

When we use words kindly,
then we will use words wisely.

175

What You Give Is What You Get

For if you forgive other people when they sin against you, your heavenly Father will also forgive you.

MATTHEW 6:14 (NIV)

The principle of forgiveness is a conditional one; we forgive others, and then God forgives us. To experience God's forgiveness, we have to be prepared to share his forgiveness with those who have trespassed against us.

It is more beneficial to receive God's forgiveness by forgiving others than harboring grudges. God pays dividends on the forgiveness we offer to others. We lose when we hold malice and resentment. Lord, we invest today. We forgive all those who hurt us along our way. Amen.

When we give others forgiveness,
we receive joy and happiness.

176

Holiness Is a Choice

For it is written: "Be holy because I am holy."
1 PETER 1:16 (NIV)

The Lord is holy. He sets the standard for morality and holds in tension, justice, and mercy. God, who is holy, calls us to be holy too. To be holy does not mean sinless but separateness. Holiness is not being without fault but in Christ's blood to seek coverage for your fault.

When we who are in a relationship with God conform to his standards, we allow his character to be formed in us. We become separated from sin and dedicated to his specific use. Let us live holy lives and dedicate ourselves to God's use. Today, I choose to be holy, Lord. Amen.

I make my choice boldly!
I will be holy!

177

Tell and Be Healed

Confess your sins to each other and pray for each other so that you may be healed.

JAMES 5:16 (NLT)

Jesus offered himself on the cross as the sacrifice for our sins. When we confess our sins to him, we receive pardon and peace. Sometimes, though, there is a need to confess our sins to others, those who we have hurt and those who have hurt us.

This confession includes sharing our struggles, offering support, and being accountable. This confession also brings healing and restores broken relationships. When we confess to one another and pray for one another, our healing will be manifested. Thank you, Jesus, for breaking the power of sin and setting the prisoner free. Amen.

To one another, let us confess,
walk in healing, and be blessed.

178

Far and Near Peace

"Peace, peace, to those far and near," says the Lord. "And I will heal them."

ISAIAH 57:19 (NIV)

Peace is never the absence of war but the presence of God in all life's circumstances, especially in wars. This presence gives holy confidence and a sense of peace that, despite the war, all will be well. This presence also means wholeness and victory.

God speaks this promise of peace to those close to him and those far removed. God offers healing from brokenness and misery. God's healing is God's peace. God at this moment is saying to you, "Peace!" Amen.

Today, God speaks his peace.
He offers healing and release.

179

By Yourself

After he had dismissed them, he went up on a mountainside by himself to pray.
MATTHEW 14:23 (NIV)

Jesus dismissed the crowd after he ended a challenging day of ministry. He was tired. He needed a place of rest and recovery. He found it on the mountainside by himself in the place of prayer.

Sometimes the nature of the task requires it to be done alone. Going solo can be a valuable experience and should be embraced as an important rendezvous that brings out the best in you. So, get comfortable with yourself, by yourself. Climb the mountain, and there pray. Thank you, Lord, for the mountaintop experiences. Amen.

Get alone with God and pray!
You will receive strength for your day.

180

You Are Protected

I will protect him because he knows my name.

PSALM 91:14 (ESV)

Knowing a person's name suggests we know that person's characteristics, personality traits, likes, and dislikes. Knowing the truth about a product prevents its abuse and misuse, insulating us and protecting us from negative, disastrous consequences.

God's name is powerful, offering protection, peace, and pardon. Knowing the truth of God's name protects us from the power of every other name that threatens us. Lord, we long to know you and the protection of your name. Amen.

Know God's name,
and you will know gain.

181

Hear and Heed

Give ear to my words, O Lord; consider my groaning. Give attention to the sound of my cry, my King and my God, for to you do I pray.

PSALM 5:1–2 (ESV)

Human beings desire attention. We desire to be loved, to be heard, to be understood. The psalmist expressed his desire to be heard. He asked God to listen to him because he was his King and Judge who executes justice on his behalf.

God honors this legitimate human need to be heard. When our words deteriorate to a sigh, he pays attention and listens to our cry. He is paying attention to you right now. Thank you, Lord, for hearing even our sighs. Amen.

God knows his own;
our sighs and groans reach God's throne.

182

Help for the Humble

The woman came and knelt before him.
"Lord, help me!" she said.

MATTHEW 15:25 (NIV)

In a moment of difficulty, this woman asked for help from the Lord. She asked because she knew he was willing and able. Some people are not willing to accept help because they view this as weakness and personal failure.

It is important for us to accept our limitations and to acknowledge our dependency and need, especially our need for God. We should also be humble and ask God for help when in need. With God, both the position of our knees and the posture of our hearts matter. Lord, with our hearts and with our knees, we bow before you. Amen.

Humility is wealth.
It guarantees God's help.

183

Never Forgotten

"What is the price of five sparrows—two copper coins? Yet God does not forget a single one of them."

LUKE 12:6 (NLT)

When we experience personal troubles and tragedies, we tend to think God has forgotten us. But God never forgets us. How do we know this? Jesus reminded his followers that God remembers sparrows.

My friend, if God took the time and the trouble to remember the sparrow, trust me, he remembers you. God is intimately aware of every minute detail that concerns you, including your hair and fingernail. You are not forgotten. God knows your name. Hallelujah! Amen.

Never feel downtrodden;
you are not forgotten.

184

Still, Rejoice

Though the fig tree does not bud and the fields produce no food,
though there are no sheep in the pen and no cattle in the stalls,
yet I will rejoice in the Lord, I will be joyful in God my Savior.

HABAKKUK 3:17–18 (NIV)

To rejoice is a deliberate decision to celebrate the good, especially in the midst of the bad. Sometimes the situations look dismal; we feel the doom and despair and see no reason to celebrate, but there always is a reason to celebrate.

God is on our side, and he will provide. He is your maker, promoter, defender, and friend. So make your decision. Rejoice in God's provision, those you have experienced and those yet to come. Thank you, Lord. Amen.

Focusing on the good
gets you over the bad.

185

Take Comfort

For the Lord has comforted his people.
He has redeemed Jerusalem.
ISAIAH 52:9 (NLT)

God gave us the gift of life. He also gave us dominion over the created order. By our reckless decision, we gave up our dominion and our ownership to another. This was a death sentence, but God determined that we should live and expended the precious resource of his Son to redeem us.

We can take comfort that God did not leave us to our own devices. He took back our dominion from the one that dominated us through the power of sin and restored it to us. The Lord comforts his people. He restores our prosperity. Thank you, Lord. Amen.

We are no longer devoured.
Thank God we are restored!

186

Firm Focus

But my eyes are fixed on you, Sovereign Lord; in you, I take refuge—do not give me over to death.
Psalm 141:8 (NIV)

Upon entering any public building, one should locate the nearest exit. An exit is a place of escape from danger. In life, we will experience storms and trouble and need a way to escape. God offers himself as the escape from life's storms.

God is the sure refuge where we can fix our eyes and hearts and run to in moments of difficulty and danger. He will protect us from the onslaught of the storm. He will not allow us to die. Lord, we look to you. Amen.

Lord, I fix my eyes on you.
You deliver from death and danger too.

187

Wait in Hope

But if we look forward to something we don't yet have, we must wait patiently.

ROMANS 8:25 (NLT)

Waiting with perseverance is waiting with patience and hope. No matter how long it takes before our hope manifests, we do not entertain the thought of giving up. We possess the conviction that we will receive the desired expectation. We keep looking for it. We keep hoping for it.

When we look in the hope, our waiting moment is not dreary with passivity or anxiety but expectant with God's ability. We know God can never fail. So we wait eagerly, Lord. Teach us. Amen.

Wait eagerly and expectantly.
Remember God is God of the suddenly.

188

Power to Witness

But you will receive power when the Holy Spirit comes upon you. And you will be my witnesses.

ACTS 1:8 (NLT)

Sugar is a powerful source of energy. As sugar is to the physical body, so is the Holy Spirit to the spiritual body. We need the power of the Holy Spirit to fulfill God's purpose on earth. The Holy Spirit energizes us and accomplishes the activity of witnessing in and through us.

When we speak, the Holy Spirit gives power to our words and convicts others of their need for Christ. The Holy Spirit gets the job done. Holy Spirit, come and use us for your glory! Amen.

Let's be God's witness
and tell of his faithfulness.

189

Only God Knows

Since you know their hearts (for you alone know every human heart).

1 KINGS 8:39 (NIV)

The human heart is capable of many deep thoughts. These thoughts are sometimes too deep for the human itself to understand, but God knows our thoughts. He knows all things. He knows what we think and why we think what we think. He knows the thoughts that give rise to fears, prejudices, attitudes, and habits good and bad.

Perhaps you are one of those people who do not understand your thoughts. Ask God to help you and search out the deep things in your heart. Search our hearts, O Lord. Amen.

God knows our hearts.
He formed every part.

190

Path Maker

I am the Lord, who opened a way through the waters, making a dry path through the sea.

ISAIAH 43:16 (NLT)

The sea is boundless. It is almost impossible to fathom its depths. As fathomless as it seems, however, it has a beginning and an ending,and God knows its beginning and its end, and yes, God knows how to make a path through the sea.

When your way seems impossible, remember that God still makes ways and paths even in the sea. He is on the sea of your life right now, making a way for you. The waters may be great, but God will make a way for you. Thank you, Lord. Amen.

God is making a way for you.
Be courageous and go through.

191

Who Is Your Master?

"No one can serve two masters."

MATTHEW 6:24 (NLT)

Most of us would rather straddle two fences and be friends with everybody than choose a side and inherit an enemy. We prefer openness in a safe place than the tension in a small space. The reality is only one person can claim our allegiance and our loyalty.

Jesus claimed that it is impossible to love the world and to love him simultaneously. We cannot be committed to his agenda and the world's agenda at the same time. So, what should we do? Let us make a choice and determine who we will serve as master. Our choice is only good if our choice is God. Lord, we choose you. Amen.

Choose Jesus as master.
You will avoid disaster.

192

Take a Rest

For anyone who enters God's rest also rests from their works, just as God did from his.

HEBREWS 4:10 (NIV)

Some people get caught up with doing and never find the time for being. They are busy constantly but are never fulfilled spiritually. God's word to those persons is rest. Center yourself in God, your Creator, and rest.

Resting allows us to enjoy the moments, the simple blessings of the day. When we enter into God's rest, we cease from our laboring, from thinking we have to do to be. My advice is simple: rest and be quiet. Lord, we rest. Amen.

God invites us to ease stress.
Let it go and be at rest.

193

Weigh In

Every way of a man is right in his own eyes, but the Lord weighs the heart.
PROVERBS 21:2 (ESV)

As human beings, we judge a situation based on what we see and what we feel is right. This tendency makes us not the best judges of character because we have not examined our motivation.

We admit that sometimes good ideas come from a wrong heart. A deed may be done because of the perceived benefit to be derived from doing it. When God weighs the heart, he examines motivation. He determines what is right. So, let's weigh in with God. Lord, we weigh in. Amen.

Let's let God weigh the hearts.
He formed them and knows every part.

194

Reason to Sing

I will sing of the steadfast love of the Lord,
forever; with my mouth, I will make known
your faithfulness to all generations.
PSALM 89:1 (ESV)

The psalmist experienced God's steadfast love. What was his response? He determined to sing about it. Like the psalmist, we have been the beneficiaries of God's steadfast love, and like him, we ought to sing.

Today, let us surrender our mouths as instruments and declare God's goodness. We sing because we are awed by God's constant love. Our unfaithfulness and our unfruitfulness place us in jeopardy, yet we are never bereft of God's love. What else can we do but sing? Accept our songs, Lord. Amen.

Your continuous, unconditional love
causes me to sing loudly and proudly.

195

Bless the Lord

Let all that I am praise the Lord; with my whole heart, I will praise his holy name.

PSALM 103:1 (NLT)

To bless is to speak well of another. It is to lift, to esteem highly, and to praise. I determined that all I am will praise the Lord. My heart, my mind, and my soul will praise God. I, therefore, speak to my soul and instruct it to bless the Lord.

How can I not bless him? My healer, deliverer, sin pardoner, burden bearer, heavy load sharer, way maker, and storm breaker. He is everything to me. Therefore, I summon every part of my being to praise him and the wonder of his matchless, high, holy, and awesome name. Now I don't have any time left to complain. Praise him! Praise him! Praise him! Amen.

I will bless God's name.
I choose to bless him again and again.

196

Eyes and Feet

My eyes are always on the Lord, for he rescues me from the traps of my enemies.

PSALM 25:15 (NLT)

Our feet follow where our eyes go. If this were not the case, we would walk backward or rather walk looking backward. This is not the case; we walk looking ahead, and our feet come behind.

To follow God then, we need to fix our eyes on him. When our eyes remain fixed on God, our feet follow where God is, and our feet are freed from every trap of the enemy. Let us ensure that our eyes are toward the Lord. Lord, keep our eyes on you. Amen.

When our eyes are on God,
our feet he guards.

197

Delight

When he said this, all his opponents were humiliated, but the people were delighted with all the wonderful things he was doing.

LUKE 13:17 (NIV)

People judge our actions because they do not understand our motives, nor do they understand our mission. Jesus's mission and motive were to usher in God's kingdom by doing good to all.

Serving Jesus requires daily commitment and cannot be limited to specified days. There will be those who seek to place limits on your ministry. Don't be distracted by them. Continue faithfully. You will give God and others delight. Help us, Lord. Amen.

Do the right and
give God delight.

198

Consider

Look at the ravens. They don't plant or harvest or store food in barns, for God feeds them.

LUKE 12:24 (NLT)

God is invested in the insignificant, such as the ravens. They are special to God. Consider that God loves you. Consider that God takes care of you. If the seeming insignificant ravens who offer a minimal contribution to God's kingdom are within his providential care, how much more you?

Be confident God will feed you; God will provide for you; God will let the light of his presence shine upon you; God will protect you. Why? You are significant to God. You are his, and you are all he has. Lord, we have considered, and you are such a wonder. Thank you. Amen!

God, it is true.
We are special to you.

199

For Me He Prays

For he bore the sin of many and made intercession for the transgressors.
ISAIAH 53:12 (NIV)

Jesus is a sin bearer and intercessor. He bore my sins on the cross. Jesus took my place. He prayed for me, a sinner, though I was undeserving of God's grace. He prayed not just for me but included you too. It was for many.

Jesus bore our sin in his body and prayed for us so we can be forgiven. We must be worthy of his prayer, for God, his Father, hears. Yes, we can do better. Yes, we can live right. Yes, we have the power to live forever in his light. Thank you, Lord. Amen.

Jesus bore the sins of many.
Give yours to him. Don't carry any.

200

Go in Peace

Again he said, "Peace be with you. As the Father has sent me, so I am sending you."
JOHN 20:21 (NLT)

Jesus came to accomplish the very difficult task of redemption. He came in obedience to his father's command. God gave him the peace, the inner strength, and the resolve to accomplish the task. He did.

Maybe you have been asked to complete a task in Christ's name, and it makes you a little uncomfortable, a little fretful. Be at peace! Remember you are on divine assignment. So go with Christ's peace. You will accomplish it. Thank you for your reassuring peace. Amen.

God's peace surrounds your steps.
With God's peace, you are forever kept.

201

It's Wiped Out

Having canceled the charge of our legal indebtedness, which stood against us and condemned us; he has taken it away, nailing it to the cross.

COLOSSIANS 2:14 (NIV)

On average, we commit three sins daily: one in the morning, one in the afternoon, and one at night. If we multiply this number by 365 days in the year, that gives an average of 995 sins annually. If we multiply this number by the number of years we have lived, we get a truer picture of sins committed.

Can you imagine those sins crying against us in God's face? Wow! What disaster! But Jesus took them out of the way, nailing them to the cross. Hallelujah! He removed them completely. Now we can go to God. We have access. Thank you, Jesus. Amen.

Rejoice, I say.
Your sins are out of the way.

202

Cleansed

But the voice answered a second time from heaven,
"What God has made clean, do not call common."
ACTS 11:9 (ESV)

Some people have difficulty seeing us the way God sees us because they think we are the total of what we were or what we did. They often judge us based on our appearance and our past. To them, we are common, nothing special.

But let us remember we are nuggets from God's gold mine, and when he cleanses us, we become the diamond that shines. He has cleansed you. Bless the Lord! Amen.

God has declared you clean
and covered you with his sheen.

203

All Is Not Lost

And one of the elders said to me, "Weep no more; behold, the Lion of the tribe of Judah, the Root of David, has conquered so that he can open the scroll and its seven seals."

REVELATION 5:5 (ESV)

Have you ever been to a place where you thought there was no hope for you, no way out of your situation? A place where you wept in despair and defeat because you were convinced that all was lost? If you ever come to such a place of hopelessness, it is important to remember that Jesus is hope.

Jesus, the conquering lion of the tribe of Judah, has already won the war. So, steady yourself in the battle, wipe your tears, and witness the victory. We wait for your salvation, Lord. Amen.

Lion of Judah, you won the victory!
Hallelujah!

204

Blessed Dead

"Write this down: Blessed are those who die in the Lord from now on … for they will rest from their hard work; for their good deeds follow them!"

REVELATION 14:13 (NLT)

Dying can be a wonderful experience if you are blessed. The dead are blessed if they die in the Lord and they have done all the duties that were required of them. Dying in the Lord is what determines whether or not you are a blessed dead.

The memory of the deeds done in Christ's name becomes the legacy left behind. These deeds are what sing your praise. So, it does not matter then where you die or how you die, but it matters in whom you die. When you die in Christ, you are forever with the Lord. Amen, so let it be!

You die secured
if you die in the Lord.

205

Come Quickly

"Yes, I am coming soon!" Amen! Come, Lord Jesus!
REVELATION 22:20 (NLT)

Jesus is coming soon, although we do not know when; Jesus promised to come back to earth again. Many get fooled into thinking that they have all the time in the world. Others say they have been waiting and there is no sign of his imminent coming. Some doubt, thinking since he has not come after two thousand years, he will not come again.

It is certain, however, that he will come, and his coming will take many people by surprise. It behooves us then to prepare ourselves and be ready for Jesus's coming. We ought to be able to say, "Come, Lord Jesus. Amen."

Let's do some preparing,
for Jesus is coming.

206

Open Door

Here I am! I stand at the door and knock. If anyone hears my voice and opens the door, I will come in and eat with that person, and they with me.
REVELATION 3:20 (NIV)

Jesus is at your heart's door, knocking. Do you not hear his voice? Jesus desires to come to make your heart his home so he can have fellowship with you. You may be facing a challenging situation and desire change. Here is your chance.

Jesus is outside waiting to come in. Are you going to open? If you let him in, his presence will change your situation. He provides the ability, identity, prosperity, and liberty—all that you need to live abundantly. Master, we open our hearts to you. Amen.

That Jesus offers himself is sure.
You only need to open the door.

207

Stay in Love

Keep yourselves in God's love as you wait for the mercy of our Lord Jesus Christ to bring you to eternal life.

JUDE 1:21 (NIV)

God gives his love without prejudice and conditions, and he challenges us to keep ourselves in his love. The decision to keep ourselves in God's love is not entirely ours, for God provides us with mercy, goodness, and grace, the tools we use to keep ourselves in his love.

As fire is maintained by poking and adding fresh coals, our lives are maintained by adding God's love. We must also be aware of such things as lack of forgiveness, selfishness, and greed, which dampen and smother the fire of God's love. We must so avoid them. Lord, help us fan the fire of your love. Amen.

Jesus shows us his mercy.
We are kept in God's love securely.

208

Give Generously

Remember this - a farmer who plants only a few seeds will get a small crop. But the one who plants generously will get a generous crop.

2 CORINTHIANS 9:6 (NLT)

There is a direct proportion between the number of seeds sown and the size of the harvest. Planting more seeds could only mean more to harvest. And planting a few seeds means less to harvest. Which kind of harvest do you prefer? I believe the answer is large.

As a wise farmer then, plant seeds of freedom, hope, love, justice, peace, kindness, forgiveness, and patience. Be generous with your sowing! You will be rewarded when reaping time comes. Lord, we release these seeds in faith. Amen.

When we are generous with seeds,
our harvest is bounteous indeed.

209

Chains Are Off

Suddenly an angel of the Lord appeared … "Quick, get up!" he said, and the chains fell off Peter's wrists.

ACTS 12:7 (NIV)

The enemy tries many things to hold us from our purpose, God's purpose. But God is always watching to ensure that his purposes are fulfilled in our lives. God's angels attend to us and bring God's Word to pass. God's angel always appears.

Like Peter, we will encounter moments of confusion and captivity. In our difficult moments, God's angel will stand by us and give us release. Therefore, the enemy's plans will be thwarted, and our chains will fall off. Hallelujah! Amen.

I make no bluff.
I declare, "Rise!" Your chains will fall off.

210

Priority

Then we apostles can spend our time in
prayer and teaching the word.
ACTS 6:4 (NLT)

The disciples were challenged with the use of their time. Should they do social ministry, or should they worship? Their decision was easy; they chose to worship.

We often spend our effort, time, and money on temporal things that offer no eternal value. We need to decide what takes priority. God's Word, God's purpose, God's agenda must take priority in our lives. Settle the conflict with the urgent and important. Cultivating a relationship with God will help us spend our time wisely. Get your fill each day of Jesus and his Word. Amen.

Be devoted to prayer.
It brings God near.

211

Title of Your Song

With praise and thanksgiving, they sang to the Lord:
"He is good; his love toward Israel endures forever."
EZRA 3:11 (NIV)

God is good to us all the time. God is good to us when we are good, and God is good to us when we are not so good. God's goodness encourages us to sing, "God is good."

Our songs are declarations of God's goodness in our lives. Our songs proclaim that God is wondrous in all his ways. Our songs are invitations to others to join in the celebration of God's goodness. Let the sound of our songs reach heaven. God is good, and his love continues forever. Amen.

Let us keep singing and
honor God with our thanksgiving.

212

Blessed by the Blesser

All praise to God, the Father of our Lord Jesus Christ, who has blessed us with every spiritual blessing in the heavenly realms because we are united with Christ.

EPHESIANS 1:3 (NLT)

God is the possessor of all things known and unknown, and God has given us every spiritual blessing in heavenly places. This means that every resource available to Christ is available to us. Every resource we need to live in this world is ours.

If Christ lived victoriously, so can we. If he had patience, so can we, and if he lived the blessed life, so can we. We must shake off the poverty spirit and embrace God's spiritual blessings. When we are united with Christ, we inherit the blessings. We have more than enough. Thank you, Lord. Amen.

The Blesser has come our way.
We are blessed today and every day!

213

Fear and Fair

Do not take advantage of each other, but fear your God. I am the Lord your God.

LEVITICUS 25:17 (NIV)

When we cultivate a reverent fear of God, we also cultivate a desire to do what pleases God. This reverential fear of God channels us in a right relationship with our brothers and sisters.

In the right relationship, we are less likely to cheat them, take advantage of them, or cause them pain and injury. If we cheat others, we cheat God and cheat ourselves out of God's blessings for us. We need to remember that we never gain when we cheat and cause our brothers and sisters pain. Lord, we fear you, and we will be fair. Amen.

Our God is near.
We will fear and be fair.

214

Not Failed, Not Forsaken

For I will be with you as I was with Moses.
I will not fail you or abandon you.

JOSHUA 1:5 (NLT)

God has promised to be with us ever and to never fail us. Other people may fail and forsake us, but God does not have that option. He guarantees his presence and his solemn pledge not to fail us.

Failing and forsaking others in need is out of character for God. That would make him changeable and unlike God. So, let's take comfort that God is with us, and because he is, we cannot fail. May the presence of the Lord fill us with strength, peace, and love. Amen.

Forsaken or failed? Never!
God is with us ever!

215

Hold Your Hope

We who have fled to take hold of the hope set before us may be greatly encouraged.

HEBREWS 6:18 (NIV)

Hope is an enabler, an equipper, an encourager, and an empowerer. Hope is the power to live when you feel like dying. It is the strength to continue when you don't feel like trying.

What affords us this hope? God himself, who is our refuge and the cause of our hope. He bids us hope. We declare we will yet hope. Whatever you do, do not let go of her hand. If you are alive, hope! Amen.

Hope is holding you;
hold to hope too!

216

Stewards Serve

Each of you should use whatever gift you have received to serve others, as faithful stewards of God's grace in its various forms.

1 PETER 4:10 (NIV)

Everyone has received at least one gift from God, thanks to God's generosity. This gift requires—even demands—responsibility. We must serve God and serve others with our gift. We were not given the gift for our use only but for service to one another.

The employment of our gift in the service to others is that which qualifies us as good stewards. What is your gift? Use it in God's service. Yes, serve and you will be served. We are at your service, Lord. Amen.

You received it freely.
Share it generously.

217

What Pleases God

Because it has pleased the Lord to make
you a people for himself.
1 SAMUEL 12:22 (ESV)

You may not have been born of a noble family or estate. You may not possess any great skill of oratory or great fortune. Yet God, by his own choice and volition, selected you and made you his people.

It is amazing to think that you could bring God pleasure. God is pleased with you and offers the guarantee to make you his special people. God is offering himself to you. Will you offer yourself to him? Please say yes. Praise the Lord, your answer is yes. Amen.

No power this truth can sever.
We are God's special treasure.

218

Strength in Grace

Do not be led away by diverse and strange teachings, for it is good for the heart to be strengthened by grace, not by foods, which have not benefited those devoted to them.

HEBREWS 13:9 (ESV)

It takes courage to acknowledge one's weakness. Through our admission of weakness and failure, we receive the strength to overcome them. You see, our admission activates grace, which releases the strength to overcome.

Grace gives the courage to trust, the power to fight, and the hope to stand strong. Grace enables us to face the foe, to persevere, and to overcome. The cure for a weak heart is grace. Grace and more grace, Lord. Amen.

Make some space
and give your heart some grace.

219

Water Rock

They were not thirsty when he led them through the desert. He divided the rock, and water gushed out for them to drink.

ISAIAH 48:21 (NLT)

Our God possesses an inexhaustible storehouse, including mountains, seas, rivers, springs, and even rocks. He is the source of all good things. With God, we have no lack because God is well able to supply all the resources we need.

Sometimes the supply may seem limited, dried up, or nonexistent, but there is always more at the source. God satisfied the children of Israel, and he will satisfy us. We must stay connected to the source to receive our supply. Let us allow God to lead us. He will lead us to never-failing springs. Oh, living waters, burst from the rock for us. Amen.

In a place of scarcity,
God can make plenty!

220

Release

Set me free from my prison, that I may praise your name.

PSALM 142:7 (NIV)

God receives no pleasure when we are victims of the forces of darkness. He sent his Son to destroy those forces so that we may walk free of Satan's power. He sets us free from our prison to praise his name. He enables us to say, "Satan had us bound, but Jesus turned our lives around."

We may recall being imprisoned and at the edge of the precipice, but Jesus set us free. Now we have every reason to give thanks and to praise his name. We have moved from prison to praise. Thank you, Father! Amen!

God set me free from prison and pain.
Now I give glory to his name.

221

Being Faithful

But you must remain faithful to the things you have been taught.
2 TIMOTHY 3:14 (NLT)

Faithfulness is a quality developed over time, through diligence, discipline, and a resolute disposition not to give up. Challenging circumstances can test our commitment, causing us to abort our mission and God-given mandate.

People also challenge us to abort purpose when we desire their approval more than God's approval and when we allow their opinions to hold more weight than God's Word. We are encouraged to be faithful and continue in the things we have learned and that we know to be true. Give us the grace to continue, Lord. Amen.

Continue therein,
and peace will flow within.

222

Reason to Praise

"Praise be to the Lord, the God of Israel because he has come to his people and redeemed them."

LUKE 1:68 (NIV)

God loves us and desires to be in a relationship with us. He sent his only Son into the world to be our Savior and Redeemer. God looks on us with favor, mercy, and love. This is the reason to give him praise.

God takes notice of us and dotes on us with much affection. We are important to him, and he comes to meet our needs. So, yes, tell him what you need today. He is only a prayer away. Start by telling him you need him. Lord, I need you. Amen.

This sacred thought I will savor:
God looks on me with favor.

223

Reward in Full

May the Lord repay you for what you have done. May you be richly rewarded by the Lord, the God of Israel, under whose wings you have come to take refuge.

RUTH 2:12 (NIV)

When one's efforts and labor are rewarded, it is a pleasant experience. The reward should not be a reason for service, and lack of reward should not be a reason to give up. We must go beyond the call of duty whether we are recognized or rewarded.

Hear the good news: the Lord will be no one's debtor. Whatever our work is, rest assured that it will be rewarded by the Lord. Please note there will be no tax or national insurance deductions; it will be a full reward. So be generous and give your best efforts. Lord, we look forward to payday. Amen.

Remember: keep working.
Payday is coming!

224

Raised from the Heap

The Lord makes poor and makes rich; he brings low and he exalts. 8He raises up the poor from the dust; he lifts the needy from the ash heap.

1 SAMUEL 2:7–8 (ESV)

The Lord is awesome and powerful. The universe and all its kings and kingdoms are at his command. Although he holds such an exalted position, he befriends the lowly and the poor and lifts them from their position.

The Lord is conscious of where you are. He knows the circumstances that led you there, and he does not condemn you. All is not lost. A new day is coming because God is getting ready to lift you to a position of power, peace, and prosperity. So we pray, Lord, lift us; help us to stand. Amen.

It is God's decision.
He will lift you to a new position.

225

Limitless Storehouse

And he will be the stability of your times, the abundance of salvation, wisdom, and knowledge; the fear of the Lord is Zion's treasure.

ISAIAH 33:6 (ESV)

The foundation of a building holds every part of the building together, giving the building strength, stability, prominence, and prestige. When we are in a relationship with God, he is the sure foundation, and he holds us together in him.

Fearing God is the key to life and the key to all resources that he possesses. God provides from his rich store of salvation, wisdom, and knowledge of all we will ever need. When we hold him, we hold all. God is indeed the best treasure to hold. Lord, help us to hold you. Amen.

When Jesus Christ is our friend,
we have treasure without end.

226

You Have a Mighty One

There the Lord will be our Mighty One. It will be like a place of broad rivers and streams.

ISAIAH 33:21 (NIV)

Sometimes situations and people overwhelm us. They intimidate us and cause us to feel small, insignificant, of lesser value, and powerless. Perhaps you have felt this way before. Hear what God says: the Lord, the mighty one, is with us.

When God is with us, he enlarges us and increases our sphere of influence. We are like the place where rivers and streams meet. We are prosperous and productive. So, lift your head, God's little one. You are in the company of the mighty one! Amen and amen.

With shouts of confidence, say,
"The mighty one is with us today!"

227

Judge and All

For the Lord are our judge, our lawgiver, and our king. He will care for us and save us.
ISAIAH 33:22 (NLT)

God operates in many portfolios: king, judge, shepherd, savior, and lawgiver. In whichever portfolio he operates, he is committed to saving me. The Lord is whoever I need him to be. I know all will be well.

God is bread when I am hungry and living water when I am thirsty. He is the righteous Savior who comes to me in moments of weakness and leads me from weakness to greatness. Bless the Lord, my judge and king. Amen.

The Lord of victory
always comes to save me.

228

Who and Do

"You shall not steal; you shall not deal falsely; you shall not lie to one another."
LEVITICUS 19:11 (ESV)

A person who claims not to be a liar may tell a white lie occasionally. A person who claims not to be a thief occasionally keeps the extra change the storekeeper overpaid. Both acts constitute dealing falsely with others.

God desires truth in our inward parts. He wants us to relate to one another with full disclosure. Half-truths are still lies, and withholding information for personal gain amounts to the same. Let us desist from such acts and radiate God's truth at all times. Help us, Lord. Amen.

Let's do the real deal.
We must not lie or steal.

229

Love Happy

It does not rejoice at wrongdoing, but rejoices with the truth.

1 CORINTHIANS 13:6 (ESV)

Love is not an empty expression but the manifestation of an individual's deep desire for the well-being of another. Love is capable of believing, bearing, hoping, and rejoicing. Love rejoices when the truth is revealed. She rejoices as an expression of deep joy.

Yes, love's joy bells go ringing when it hears truth telling. We are challenged to tell the truth if telling the truth places us in a bad light or makes us lose credibility. We must, however, speak the truth as an act of love. May our lives reflect truth today and every day. Amen.

Let's speak the truth by choice.
Then love will rejoice!

230

Now I Am Well

No one living in Zion will say, "I am ill;" and the sins of those who dwell there will be forgiven.

ISAIAH 33:24 (NIV)

There are many times when our hearts are heavy, burdened with guilt and shame. The sick, heavy, sinking feeling is usually symptomatic of the presence of sin—both unconfessed and unforgiven. Sin saps the joy out of our marrow and makes us ill.

Today, we are invited to make a choice. We are invited to go to God to have our sins forgiven. Forgiveness will remove the sinking, ill feeling. Then we shall be able to say we are not ill but well. Thank you for forgiveness, Lord. Amen.

God's Word is revealed.
We choose to be healed.

231

Still Looking

"I looked for someone among them who would build up the wall and stand before me in the gap on behalf of the land so I would not have to destroy it, but I found no one."

EZEKIEL 22:30 (NIV)

God is looking for faithful people who will stand in the gap, unite in their efforts to resist evil, and restore righteousness in the land. Religious rituals cannot achieve this goal. Only hearts that have been renewed by the power of God and reconstructed by the Holy Spirit can accomplish this.

The attitude and the activity of prayer are needed to rebuild the wall that has been broken in the land. So, stand in the gap and pray for God's mercy and favor upon the land. God will stay his hand and save our land. Lord, we avail ourselves to you. Help us stand, Lord. Amen.

Brother, sister, stand in the gap.
Rescue the land from sin's awful trap!

232

Bad Power

Woe to those who devise wickedness … because it is in the power of their hand.
MICAH 2:1 (ESV)

Power does not give us the right or the clearance to do wrong just because we can and because we are strong. That is bad power. A correct assessment of power makes us aware that when power is abused, there are consequences for both the abused and the abuser.

God has declared war on those who abuse power. He warns that there are negative consequences for those who practice wickedness. So let us not abuse power but keep the focus right and do what's right. Help us, Lord. Amen.

Today, take a stand!
Don't abuse the power in your hand.

233

No Harm, Neighbor

Do not plan evil against your neighbor,
who dwells trustingly beside you.
PROVERBS 3:29 (ESV)

Our neighbors depend upon us for covering, camaraderie, and caring concern. They entrust themselves to us as they commandeer themselves to care for us. We then, who are appointed for their defense, must protect them.

As God's people, we must never use our neighbors' dependency and vulnerability to plot their demise or disaster. Our words and actions must enhance their well-being and welfare. May God increase our capacity to be more neighborly. Amen.

Others we must not harm. Remember,
let's be a covering and a balm.

234

Searching for Sheep

"For this is what the Sovereign Lord says: I myself will search for my sheep and look after them."
EZEKIEL 34:11 (NIV)

It is amazing how sheep can get scattered in a moment of fright. Orderly mannered sheep can run helter-skelter in all directions in the presence of an attacker.

God is aware of the attackers that scatter his sheep to dangerous places. He promises to seek them out in the ravines and other places where they have been scattered. God will look for them. God will look for you, too, wherever you may have wondered. He will take care of you. Thank you, Father. Amen.

You were scattered.
Praise God! you will be gathered.

235

Equal Measure

"With the measure you use, it will be measured to you—and even more."

MARK 4:24 (NIV)

Natural law suggests that our gain is proportionate to our giving. If we give in small measures, our gain is small. If we give in moderate measures, our gain is moderate. If we give in large measures, our gain is great.

It follows then if we desire more, we must be prepared to give more. Our desire to get more must be fueled by a passion to give more. Perhaps the time has come to disband the spoonful measurements of giving. Let's use shovels. Increase our capacity, Lord. Amen.

Measure with shovels; disband spoons.
Get ready. An increase is coming soon.

236

Faith Rest

I did this so you would trust not in human wisdom but the power of God.

1 CORINTHIANS 2:5 (NLT)

Each of us is tempted to rest our faith in what we can see rather than what we cannot see. We operate better when we are sure of something we can see and touch. We rest our faith on methods and standards we have tested and proven. Although these standards may be humanly sure, they may not be divinely secured.

So let us be God sure and divinely secured. We end our reliance on human power and rest in God's power because God's power never fails. God is the all-powerful and all-wise God. He is our sure foundation. Lord, we rest our faith on the good foundation. Amen.

Every moment and every hour,
rest your faith on Christ's power.

237

Full Face

I will no longer hide my face from them, for I will pour out my Spirit on the people of Israel, declares the Sovereign Lord.

EZEKIEL 39:29 (NIV)

Parents often withhold information from their children because they are convinced it would be damaging and too much for them to handle, based on their level of maturity. God as our father is protective of us.

There comes a time in every relationship when full disclosure is necessary. God, as a loving parent, pours out his Spirit of revelation on us, which enables us to see him as he is. Thank you, Lord, for your willingness to reveal yourself to us. Amen.

God will no longer hide his face.
Oh, what grace.

238

Sovereign Silence

Be silent before the Sovereign Lord, for the day of the Lord is near.

ZEPHANIAH 1:7 (NIV)

Silence is powerful and therapeutic, but some people are afraid of it. Interestingly, we humans have one tongue and two ears, yet we talk more and listen less.

The sovereign God, omnipotent in power and omniscient in wisdom, is near us. He desires to speak to us, but we must be in a position to hear and listen. God only speaks when we are silent. In the business of our day, let us pause and be silent before God. Help us, Lord. Amen.

The adage *silence is golden* is true.
Be silent, and let God speak to you.

239

Under God's Hand

And the hand of the Lord was upon me there.
And he said to me, "Arise, go out into the
valley, and there I will speak with you."
EZEKIEL 3:22 (ESV)

Have you ever desired to speak to someone and it was not the right place or time? Effective communication takes place in a conducive atmosphere where distractions and noise are limited. God looks for such a secluded place where he can speak to you uninhibitedly.

God desires to speak to you! So, move from the place of distraction and go to a quiet place where you can hear God. Go into the valley, choose the place, and make some space for God. What are you still doing sitting? Amen.

Get up. Go into the valley.
God will speak to you there clearly.

240

My Assignment Is Worship

And he said to them, "I am a Hebrew, and I fear the Lord, the God of heaven, who made the sea and the dry land."

JONAH 1:9 (ESV)

Knowing who we are helps us to know our purpose and what we are called to do. Jonah knew he was God's prophet. In rebellion, he boarded a ship headed in the opposite direction to avoid his assignment. Yet, there, God found him.

Jonah identified himself and declared his purpose: "I am a Hebrew, and I worship the God of heaven." Like Jonah, we are people of God, and we were born for worship. No rebellion, no walking away from God's plan can revoke God's call and purpose for our lives. We are worshippers, so let us worship. Help us, Lord. Amen.

Lord, we worship right now!
At your feet, we humbly bow.

241

Seek to Live

Now, this is what the Lord says to the family of Israel: "Come back to me and live!"

AMOS 5:4 (NLT)

Human beings tend to become carried away with gifts and walk away from the giver. We get excited about the gift—to the neglect of the giver. We often walk away from God, who is the giver of every good and perfect gift.

We must remember that the giver is more important than the gift. The gifts may become broken and used up, but the giver is always there, ready to replenish and restore. We must therefore seek God the giver and not the gifts. Lord, help us to seek you. Amen.

Lord, we come back to you and live.
Your grace and mercy do give.

242

Lighted Lamps

At that time I will search Jerusalem with lamps and punish those who are complacent, who are like wine left on its dregs, who think. "The Lord will do nothing, either good or bad."

ZEPHANIAH 1:12 (NIV)

You may remember a time when you were dressed inappropriately, and you hoped others would not recognize you, but alas they did. Much to your chagrin, they made others aware of your inadequacies.

God searches us out, and nothing about us escapes his notice. God is intimately aware of everything concerning us. Let us not be found complacent, thinking anything goes. He is aware, and in the presence of his lighted lamps, we will be judged. Help us, Lord. Amen.

Some not so nice ways I see in me.
"O Lord," I cry, "remember mercy."

243

Look for God

Seek the Kingdom of God above all else, and live righteously, and he will give you everything you need.
MATTHEW 6:33 (NLT)

A group of young people were asked what they wanted in life. They answered: money, a good job, a good education, houses, fame, the fine things in life, and their list continued. They were prepared to do whatever it took to achieve their goals.

The simple truth is if we seek first the kingdom of God, all these other desires the Lord will fulfill. Yes, he gives them to us when we do his will. Seeking God first gets us everything. So, let us seek God, and we will have all we need. Help us, Lord. Amen.

Don't seek for things.
Seek God and get everything.

244

Just Call

"I called out to the Lord, out of my distress, and he answered me; out of the belly of Sheol I cried, and you heard my voice."

JONAH 2:2 (ESV)

Jonah's disobedience landed him in a place of distress, the belly bottom of a fish. He could not sink any lower. He was in the grave. In his place of distress, Jonah called on the Lord.

Jonah could have decided not to call. He could have thought he was undeserving of God's grace; he deserved what he got and really should die. Instead, he just called. Maybe all of the above is true for us, but God is simply waiting for us to call. So just call, and God will listen and respond. Thank you, Lord. Amen.

Always make mercy your plea!
From the pit, God will set you free!

245

Awesome God

The Lord will be awesome against them … and to him shall bow down, each in its place, all the lands of the nations.

ZEPHANIAH 2:11 (ESV)

God is awesome, excellent, gracious, and extravagant in his dealings with humankind. The nation of Judah had been mocked and taunted by her neighbors for her faith in God. Here God makes Judah aware that he had heard the insults and he would intervene awesomely on their behalf.

Sometimes we, too, are mocked for our faith in God, but God will show himself awesome on our behalf. Then all who see the acts of our God will worship him. Show yourself, mighty Lord, and let the earth worship. Amen.

Lord, show yourself true
and let the nations worship you.

246

Blessings Take Over

"The time will come," says the Lord, "when the grain and grapes will grow faster than they can be harvested."

AMOS 9:13 (NLT)

The economic downturn in the world's economies has caused many Christians to think that this time of scarcity is outside of God's control. The people in Amos's day encountered similar challenges. The Lord spoke in their situation as he speaks in ours now.

A time of abundance is again coming when we won't be able to harvest all that our fields will produce. Blessings will take over our lives. I am ready for those times. Are you? Until then, prepare the soil. Ready it by planting the crops. Water it with prayers, and then let's wait on God. Amen.

From planting never cease;
the Lord will give the increase.

247

Glory Facedown

So I got up and went out to the plain. And the glory of the Lord was standing there, like the glory I had seen by the Kebar River, and I fell facedown.

EZEKIEL 3:23 (NIV)

God's glory is a heavy, majestic, glorious presence that can pull us down to our knees. Ezekiel felt this weighty pressure and acknowledged his helplessness before God, falling facedown in his presence.

Sometimes our popularity, prosperity, and physical power blind us to the truth that we are helpless before God. Nothing we do in our power amounts to much before God. We must yield to him. Like this great prophet, let us fall before God. Remember, when we bow before God, we will always stand before humans. Amen and amen.

Lord, we fall at your feet,
bowing at your mercy seat.

248

When God Arises

Rise, O God, and scatter your enemies. Let those who hate God run for their lives.

PSALM 68:1 (NLT)

It is stupid to stand in front of a tsunami wave and somehow hope it will pass you by. God's power and might are of tsunami proportion. When God comes, his enemies are left without an alternative. They are scattered.

When God arises, his enemies flee before his presence. He comes in the situations and circumstances of our lives to address difficulties and impossibilities. When God comes to us, we watch our enemies scatter and disappear. Come, Lord. Come. Amen.

Lord Jesus, come today.
Scatter my enemies away.

249

All God

But God has helped me to this very day; so I stand here and testify to small and great alike.

ACTS 26:22 (NIV)

We do not readily acknowledge we need help. We give the impression we made a solo journey in our strength. We feel that admittance is a weakness. Paul, however, boldly acknowledged that God had helped him.

He was not afraid or ashamed; neither did he care what other people thought about him. Paul declared, "I am here because of God's help." Like Paul, we, too, can acknowledge all that we are we owe to God. Tell it to the little and to the large: God has been good to you! Thank you, Lord. Amen.

It is OK to say
someone helped you and showed you the way.

250

Protected

And the gracious hand of our God protected us and saved us from enemies and bandits along the way.

EZRA 8:31 (NLT)

We can count on God's protection when we travel our life's journey. Whether the journey takes us along level or treacherous paths, God's hand covers us.

Nehemiah experienced God's hand of protection traveling dangerous paths from Babylon to Jerusalem. When our enemies are waiting to ambush us and rob us of our resources, we, too, can count on God's hand of power to protect us. Wherever we travel today, the Lord's hand of protection covers our way. Bless the Lord, Amen.

In places of adversity,
God offers divine security.

251

Easy Blessings

Blessed are those who have regard for the weak;
the Lord delivers them in times of trouble.
PSALM 41:1 (NIV)

God has regard for weak, vulnerable, and lowly things. When we offer compassionate concerns for those who are weak and vulnerable, blessings accompany our lives. Not only are we blessed for success, but we are also assured of the Lord's deliverance in times of trouble.

Let us continue to help the needy and share our strength with the weak. Remember, we are blessed when we help those who are in need. I hope you want some easy blessings. Help somebody today. Amen.

Make it your daily creed
to help someone in need.

252

I Shall Not Leave

"As surely as the Lord lives and you yourself live, I won't go home unless you go with me." So Elisha returned with her.

2 KINGS 4:30 (NLT)

Through Elisha's prophetic word, the Shunammite woman had given birth to a son; now her son was dead. She knew only the prophet Elisha could remedy the situation. The Shunammite woman apprehended Elisha and requested his assistance. Elisha offered to send his servant to deal with the matter, but the woman demanded that he address the matter.

The Shunammite woman was prepared to remain in God's presence until she received his personal touch. Like her, we must be willing to stay in God's presence until he touches us personally. Teach us to stay, Lord. Amen.

Lord, this is life's essence,
to be in your presence.

253

Corner Covered

"I am Ruth, your servant. Spread your wings over your servant, for you are a redeemer."
RUTH 3:9 (ESV)

Ruth followed Naomi's advice and in secret made her way to Boaz's threshing floor. She invited Boaz to spread the corner of his garment over her! It was common custom and practice for a servant to lay at the feet of the master and share part of the covering. Shared covering meant protection and provision.

The covering from Boaz, her kinsman-redeemer, meant he was willing to provide for her as his own family, which could mean that he would marry her himself. Boaz did right by his family. Like Boaz, let us do the best for our families. Help us, Lord. Amen.

In times of challenge and adversity,
remain committed to our families.

254

Eyes on You

Behold, the eye of the Lord is on those who fear him, on those who hope in his steadfast love.

PSALM 33:18 (ESV)

"Nobody knows the trouble we bear" are words we often echo. It is quite true that other people may not be fully aware of our daily struggles. Let me introduce you to someone who is. The Lord is aware of your predicament. Yes, someone sees your situation.

The Lord's eyes are on you, and he is aware of your present situation. His eyes are on you not simply to make a mental note. God intervenes in your situations and works them in your favor. So yes, continue to hope in him, in his unfailing love. Help is near. Amen.

God's eyes are on you,
and he will see you through.

255

Can-Do God

"I know that you can do anything, and no one can stop you."

JOB 42:2 (NLT)

It is wonderful to come to a place of assurance that God can do all things. This gives you the freedom to trust in him. When you trust, you worry less and worship more. You wait for God's plans to come to pass in your life. You are confident that there is nothing that can stop the fulfillment of God's plan and purpose.

When things look impossible and you are in the midst of your pain, you can smile, knowing that God will work it out for you. So place those plans that you have before God and leave them to his able working. Thank you, God, for working them out! Amen.

Lord, all my life's plans,
I place them in your hands.

256

Ahead of You

But be assured today that the Lord your God is the one who goes across ahead of you like a devouring fire.
DEUTERONOMY 9:3 (NIV)

God walks ahead of his children. In the fire, in the flood, in bad times and in good, God walks with us. Wherever you are called to walk today, God has walked that way before. Like a devouring fire, he burns up the enemies before him.

God devours every danger that lurks along the path, allowing you to walk fearlessly. Dangers hidden and seen have no power to touch you. So fear not, but walk well under God's authority and God's covering. Amen.

God goes ahead of you,
removing dangers
so you can walk through.

257

Speak On

My tongue will proclaim your righteousness,
your praises all day long.
PSALM 35:28 (NIV)

Our tongues are in the habit of speaking whatever words they wish. For most people, a typical day no doubt includes words of criticism, slander, idle chatter, ridicule, and the list goes on. It takes a deliberate and disciplined choice to speak words of righteousness.

Like the psalmist, let us challenge our tongues to speak righteousness and praise to God. Let praise be our song, and let our tongues sing all day long. Tongues, we command you to praise the Lord! Amen.

I declare your tongue blessed
to speak words of righteousness.

258

Come and Listen

And Joshua said to the people of Israel, "Come here and listen to the words of the Lord your God."
JOSHUA 3:9 (ESV)

Our world is a busy one, and there are many concerning situations that demand our attention throughout the day. We get carried away with our tasks and fail to find the time to hear God speak. Our best and noblest task is to follow the instructions Joshua gave to the Israelites. Come and listen to the words of God.

Joshua understood that God desired to speak to the people. He understood, too, that it would be more beneficial for us to hear God's Word and receive direction and guidance for the day. So, put your day on pause. Hear what God has to say to you. Amen.

Lord, I am listening.
Speak in my sleeping
and waking.

259

Groanings

Let the groans of the prisoners come before you; according to your great power, preserve those doomed to die!

PSALM 79:11 (ESV)

Most of us are familiar with groaning. It is pain too deep for words. It is good news that our groans reach the ears of the Lord. When they do, God intervenes in the circumstances to save.

Right now, you may feel imprisoned, and your punishment may be your just reward, but God will hear your groan and have mercy. God's ears are sensitized to your unique groaning sounds. Keep groaning. God who hears is committed to helping you. Thank you, Lord. Amen.

Umm, my Lord!
Woe, my Lord!

260

Touch Not

May the Lord judge between you and me. And may the Lord avenge the wrongs you have done to me, but my hand will not touch you.

1 SAMUEL 24:12 (NIV)

All of us have been attacked at some point in our lives. The learned human response in such situations is to fight and defend oneself. Under those circumstances, it is difficult to exercise restraint.

David determined he had done no wrong to King Saul, who hunted him down like a dog. When presented with the opportunity to avenge himself, he said, "Let the Lord determine who is wrong. Let the Lord judge." Like David, let us refrain from touching our enemies. You touch them, Lord. Amen.

I will not touch
in anger or disgust.
Let the Lord touch, and it will be just.

261

Don't Be Afraid

"Don't be afraid of them. Remember the Lord, who is great and awesome, and fight for your families, your sons and your daughters, your wives, and your homes."

NEHEMIAH 4:14 (NIV)

I wish I could say that I am not afraid of anything or anyone. The truth is I do fear because my enemies are formidable. Yet, regardless of how my enemies look or what strength they carry, I am commanded not to be afraid of them.

Instead, I am to remember the Lord, who is great and awesome. I must choose not to look at my enemy but to look at God, who can deliver me from the enemy and destroy the enemy. I will remember to look up to God and refuse to fear. Amen.

I choose to remember God's power.
To him, all my enemies must surrender.

262

Pay Your Vows

"When you make a vow to the Lord your God, be prompt in fulfilling whatever you promised him. For the Lord, your God demands that you promptly fulfill all your vows, or you will be guilty of sin."

DEUTERONOMY 23:21 (NLT)

When we feel pressured and are between a rock and a hard place, we often bargain with God. We say, "God if you help us out, we vow to serve you." What tends to happen, however, is that God helps out of our situation, and we fail to pay our vows to God.

Failure to keep our promises and vows is tantamount to sin. So, let us challenge ourselves to pay our vows and keep our promises. So, pay up! Lord, give us strength. Amen.

So much is at stake.
Let's keep the promises we make.

263

Serve in Your Presence

So the Lord said to Moses, "Take Joshua the son of Nun, a man in whom is the Spirit, and lay your hand on him."
NUMBERS 27:18 (ESV)

Service is the duty of everyone. God, through his Holy Spirit, anoints us for service. We never serve in isolation but the community. Thus, the elders in our community are encouraged to lay hands on those chosen for service and affirm them.

When God's Spirit is in us, God downloads his heart to us so we can accomplish his purposes. The Spirit equips and empowers us to serve. Then he affirms us in the community where we serve. Let us honor those who serve God and serve us. We thank you for those who serve, Lord. Amen.

Give them strength and nerve
and your spirit to serve.

264

Sons of God

Behold, children are a heritage from the Lord, the fruit of the womb a reward.

PSALM 127:3 (ESV)

Receiving an inheritance is usually a time of joy. We are excited by the money or other tangible things that become our possession. Interestingly, sons and daughters are our inheritance from God. God gives children as a reward.

Managing God's heritage is a serious responsibility. We must be careful to engage their inquisitive minds and trusting spirits. We must shape their future so that they become sons and daughters of God. Help us to be good stewards of your inheritance, Lord. Amen.

Thanks we give to you, Lord!
We are grateful for your reward.

265

Peaceful Land

"I will grant peace in the land, and you will lie down and no one will make you afraid."
LEVITICUS 26:6 (NIV)

Nearly every day, there are news reports of people's rights being violated, perversions of justice, and pollution of the land with blood. Consequently, the peace of our homes and communities is threatened, and so is the peace in our personal lives. We experience fear, which is simply a by-product of the lack of peace.

We need to cry, "O for our land to have peace! Give peace to the land, Lord." God offers us this peace and the capacity to possess our souls in peace. We speak your peace, Lord. Amen.

Lord, speak your word of command
and give peace to our land.

266

Training

Discipline your children, for in that there is hope;
do not be a willing party to their death.
PROVERBS 19:18 (NIV)

Most people associate discipline with negative punishment, but it should rightfully be regarded as instruction and training in righteousness. When we take the time to instruct children, we give them the capacity to make the right choices, without which children are apt to make negative choices that can lead to disastrous consequences.

The writer of Proverbs challenges us to discipline our children. Discipline gives life and hope. If we fail to discipline our children, we participate directly in their downfall. Lord, give parents the wisdom to bring up their children. Amen.

Discipline our children right.
Let them walk in God's light.

267

Watch Your Steps

As you enter the house of God, keep your ears open and your mouth shut. It is evil to make mindless offerings to God.
ECCLESIASTES 5:1 (NLT)

God's presence is awesome and demands an attitude of holy reverence. This attitude should accompany us when we go to God's house, when we open his Word, and when we listen to him. Our willingness to listen indicates that we recognize God's sovereignty and choose to worship his majesty.

God is all-wise, loving, and gracious, and as his creation, we cannot give God orders. So, in reverence and full attention, let us be quiet and listen to what he has to say. When he speaks, we will benefit from his wise counsel. Lord, we are ready to listen. Amen.

I shut my mouth and open my ears.
Humbly, God, I offer my prayers.

268

Preferred Status

I would rather be a doorkeeper in the house of my God than dwell in the tents of wickedness.

PSALM 84:10 (ESV)

The psalmist affirms that he prefers a doorkeeper status at God's house than to have a residency with sinners. He would not allow anyone or anything to entice him or draw him away from God's house to the tents of wickedness.

Like the psalmist, when we state our preferred position, we also state the position we do not desire. Declaring our preferred position is also giving our self-definition. Now we must be determined and not move from our preferred position. Lord, fix our feet and heart in your house. Amen.

Serve as a doorkeeper
and dwell in God's house forever.

269

Fruitful

I will turn to you and make you fruitful and multiply you and will confirm my covenant with you.

LEVITICUS 26:9 (ESV)

When God impregnates us with the aroma of himself, we can only be fruitful. God places the stamp of approval and blessing upon our lives, multiplies us, and makes our lives fruitful in whatever we do.

We are not worthy of God's blessings. Neither do we qualify for it, but God gives it anyway. God is faithful and keeps his promise and covenant with us. There is no stopping us when God's hand of blessing is on our lives. Thank you for multiplying your people and making us fruitful, Lord. Amen.

God multiplies us beyond measure.
And we become God's fruitful treasure.

270

Friends

A friend is always loyal.

PROVERBS 17:17 (NLT)

The greatest evidence of a genuine friend is that he or she loves at all times. Love, when examined, is not a feeling but a decision to ensure the welfare of an individual. A friend is called to love in good and bad times, when it is easy to do so and when it is not so easy.

Being loyal is a characteristic of this true friend who is available in times of distress, misunderstandings, personal struggles, and even rejection. A loyal friend lifts you, is on your side, forgives your failings, affirms your value, and loves you to the end. Thank you, Lord, for loyal friends. Amen.

I choose to be a genuine friend.
I choose to love to the end.

271

Kept Love

I will maintain my love for him forever, and
my covenant with him will never fail.
PSALM 89:28 (NIV)

Anything that is of value needs to be maintained. Homes, structures, cars, human bodies, and relationships need to be maintained. Proper maintenance preserves the integrity, stability, and security and prevents any compromise.

Reports of broken relationships, betrayals, and lost love bemoans love that was not nurtured, nourished, or kept. We can learn from our Father God, who has given his solemn oath and promise. He will maintain his love. He will keep his covenant. He will be constant with his love. God's love for us can never be lost. Hallelujah!

Some things we cannot prove.
We can count on God's love.

272

Lands Sing

All the lands are at rest and at peace; they break into singing.

ISAIAH 14:7 (NIV)

Did you know that land can sing? Yes, that is news to me too. But it seems that when the land has rest and peace, it bursts into song. I wonder what the words of that song are. Perhaps they go something like this:

> It is a good day; my land is blessed.
> I have come through the storms
> and have passed the test.
> With prosperity and increase,
> I now am at peace.
> From violence I can rest;
> my land is truly blessed.

Do you have rest? What are the words of your song? I have peace. I am blessed. Amen

Lord, in you I rest.
I have peace, and I am blessed.

273

Free Life

Thus says the Lord of hosts, the God of Israel: Amend your ways and your deeds, and I will let you dwell in this place.

JEREMIAH 7:3 (ESV)

No one has been exempted from the evil influence of the world. Everyone has succumbed to the negative influence of sin and its subsequent death sentence. There is an alternative, however.

Jeremiah challenges us. Amend our ways. If we change our ways and deeds and return to God, he will revoke the death sentence and allow us to live. The clock is ticking, and the now moment we are assured of is passing. Repent, reform, and turn back to God's norm. Help us, Lord. Amen.

Repent by God's grace.
Then you will live in this place.

274

My God

O Lord, you are my God; I will exalt you; I will praise your name, for you have done wonderful things, plans formed of old, faithful and sure.

ISAIAH 25:1 (ESV)

My God, I praise your holy and majestic name.
With joy, I will praise you; your faithfulness I will proclaim.
You do wondrous things that fill my heart with awe.
You are my source. From you, my life, I draw.
You are faithful and sure.
You are God forevermore.
Thank you for being my God. Amen.

Remember, God makes awesome plans.
Our lives are in your hands.

275

Stuck-On Friend

There are "friends" who destroy each other, but a real friend sticks closer than a brother.

PROVERBS 18:24 (NLT)

Have you ever had anyone positively stuck on you? In a healthy relationship, it is a good thing. You can count on this friend being there, just simply showing they care. This person sticks to you because of what he or she can give. This is a real, stuck-on friend.

Some friends are in relationships because of what they can get. If they feel they are receiving nothing, they leave. These are fair-weather friends. What kind of friend are you? Stuck on or fair-weather? Be a loyal friend and get stuck on, my friend. Lord, stick to me where I need to be stuck. Amen.

Be a stuck-on friend
and stay on the journey to life's end.

276

Long Life

May you live to see your children's children.

PSALM 128:6 (NIV)

Most parents desire to see their children's children. It is a pure, euphoric joy to see the creation of the next generation and to know you had something to do with it. Grandparents often boast, "This is my grandbaby," and that's a wonderful blessing.

Here God promises us that we will be afforded this awesome privilege. This is not for mere bragging rights but the responsibility to inculcate values and morals that will positively affect the next generation. May we live to bring our children's children to you, Lord. Amen.

Our children's children are blessings.
They are the reason for rejoicing.

277

Do Good

Do not take advantage of a hired worker who is poor and needy, whether that worker is a fellow Israelite or a foreigner residing in one of your towns ... they may cry to the Lord against you, and you will be guilty of sin.

DEUTERONOMY 24:14–15 (NIV)

In the law of the jungle, the survival of the fittest is the norm. But in God's divine order, the fittest have the responsibility to care for the infirmed. The poor have a voice and an authentic place with the Lord.

The Lord listens when the poor raise their voice to God for justice, and that could mean trouble for the abuser. So here is the deal: treat everyone fairly and justly. Remember, when we take advantage of others, we lose our advantage with God. Help us, Lord. Amen.

Remember the poor and needy.
Show them love and mercy.

278

Strength

They were just trying to intimidate us, imagining that they could discourage us and stop the work. So I continued the work with even greater determination.

NEHEMIAH 6:9 (NLT)

Discouragement is a part of life's realities. When it happens, it can sap our energy and leave us too weak to fight anymore. We then entertain thoughts of giving up. Rather than give up, we can pray like Nehemiah, "Lord, strengthen my hands for the work." God heard Nehemiah's prayer and answered him.

God will also hear our prayer and give us strength in our moments of weakness. Be encouraged. Call out to God, and God will answer! He will give you his strength. Lord, give us strength. Amen.

Here is some encouragement.
God's power with you is present.

279

Resting

And the Spirit of the Lord shall rest upon him, the Spirit of wisdom and understanding, the Spirit of counsel and might, the Spirit of knowledge and the fear of the Lord.

ISAIAH 11:2 (ESV)

The Spirit of God is full of wisdom, understanding, skilled counsel, and power. He indwells the believer and makes available all his resources. The evidence of the Spirit's presence is the ability to give counsel and power.

This power is the creative energy that enables God's words and works to be accomplished. The Spirit continues to seek a place where he may rest in his power and might. Are you open to him resting on you? Say, "Rest on me, Lord." Amen.

Rest on me, Lord, every space fill.
Lead me in your power to do your will.

280

Watched Over

As I have watched over them to pluck up and break down, to overthrow, destroy, and bring harm, so I will watch over them to build and to plant, declares the Lord.

JEREMIAH 31:28 (ESV)

God is a serious contractor and builder. Sometimes this involves tearing down, uprooting, and planting. He is on the job right now in your life, building beautiful structures. God is watching over us, bringing to pass his plans and purposes.

Yes, God is orchestrating his will by accomplishing his purpose in your life. You may not think anything is happening to you, because all appears impossible. But rest assured that God is watching, covering, protecting, and nurturing his Word over your life. All is not lost. God will get it done, no matter the cost. Amen.

God watches over what concerns you and me,
now and in eternity.

281

Don't Start

Starting a quarrel is like breaching a dam; so drop the matter before a dispute breaks out.

PROVERBS 17:14 (NIV)

Many people are serving prison sentences because of a quarrel. A quarrel increases the chances of greater conflict. It always takes two to quarrel. The Bible says that starting a quarrel is like breaching a dam. When the dam is breached, there is no turning back the forces of the waters of hatred, anger, and violence. It destroys everything in its path, leaving behind the trail of brokenness.

Since we know the power of a breached dam and that we are at risk in the wake of its bursting waters, we have the responsibility to stop the quarrel before it starts. May we never give room to quarrel. Amen.

Quarrels tear families apart,
so stop one before it starts.

282

Joy Gives Strength

"Don't be dejected and sad, for the joy of the Lord is your strength!"
NEHEMIAH 8:10 (NLT)

The natural processes of life, its ups and downs, cause pain and loss. We grieve; we experience weakness and faint under the stress of the ordeal. The above text tells us about joy from the Lord's strength. When we turn our minds to God and away from the situation, a different story becomes our experience. Our grief is replaced with the joy of God's grace.

Think about the goodness of the Lord and how he restores our souls, and be encouraged. Sing and dance and allow a new level of joy to rise within. With God's strength in us and with God on our side, we are strong. Thank you for your strength, Lord. Amen.

God's strength is true.
We will make it through.

283

By the Roads

"Stand by the roads, and look, and ask for the ancient paths, where the good way is; and walk in it."
JEREMIAH 6:16 (ESV)

Although the right path for us to live has been marked out by God, many refuse to follow God's path and instead create their own. They follow a path that often leads to disaster, destruction, and death.

Today, we stand by the roads and see the good path, God's path. Do we follow God's path that has been tested and proven? Or do we create our own, using human wisdom that is bound to fail? Let us not be misled; the only path to peace and happiness is God's prescribed path. Follow it. Teach me to follow after you. Amen.

Show me the good and worn path.
I will follow with all my heart.

284

God Alone

"You are the Lord, you alone. You have made heaven, the heaven of heavens, with all their host, the earth and all that is on it, the seas and all that is in them; and you preserve all of them; and the host of heaven worships you."

NEHEMIAH 9:6 (ESV)

God has revealed himself as Father, Son, and Holy Spirit. He is the Creator and Sustainer of the universe. He alone gives life.

This life giver offers us his life. He gives life to all the dead circumstances and situations of our lives. He is worthy of our worship. As created beings, we stand in awe of him. We join with the hosts of heaven to worship you, holy God. Yes, we join the rest of the created order and cry, "You alone are the Lord." Amen.

God, you are the only life giver;
you are full of love and power.

285

Sealed Heart

Place me like a seal over your heart, like a seal on your arm; for love is as strong as death.

SONG OF SOLOMON 8:6 (NIV)

The marriage relationship ought to be one where the spouse's heart is open to the other and closed to everyone else. This can only happen if both people place the other as the seal on their hearts and their arms. Sealing keeps out intruders and locks each other in. If nurtured properly, this sealed love will weather every storm and will only be interrupted by death.

All our relationships can benefit from similar sealing. Do you agree? Let us offer them to God. Father, we offer to you all our relationships; sanctify and seal them for your glory. Amen.

When heart and arm are sealed,
God's purpose is revealed.

286

Laughter Is Good Medicine

A cheerful heart is good medicine, but a crushed spirit dries up the bones.

PROVERBS 17:22 (NIV)

I visited a friend who had been ill, both emotionally and physically. We did not talk much about God but reminisced about life, the adventures of our childhood, and the discoveries we made together. My ill friend laughed uncontrollably and continuously throughout the visit. By the time the visit ended, an hour later, my friend's spirit was lifted. She was well again.

I do affirm laughter is indeed medicine for the soul. Let us take the time to laugh and share this medicine of laughter with every crushed, broken soul. Lord, let me laugh long and loud. Give us your joy, Lord. Amen.

Laugh to your heart's delight.
Laugh both day and night.

287

Dread Warrior

But the Lord is with me as a dread warrior; therefore, my persecutors will stumble; they will not overcome me.

JEREMIAH 20:11 (ESV)

You probably can recall times when people and situations came against you to destroy you. Perhaps you had many close calls, but every time, you triumphed over them. Have you ever wondered why? Here's the reason: the Lord was with you like a dread warrior. He made your persecutors stumble.

God will fight your battles for you. God will defend your life. Your enemies' plots will fail, so they will not prevail. Like you, I can affirm I am still standing because God has always been my protector, my dread warrior. Praise God! Amen.

The mighty warrior can never fail.
His will, his Word, must prevail.

288

Hope for Zion

Zion shall be redeemed by justice and those in her who repent, by righteousness.

ISAIAH 1:27 (ESV)

Zion is a name symbolic of God's presence. It is the city where God dwells, and because God is present, certain blessings will automatically be experienced. There will be peace in the soul, prosperity and life that is whole, power to save and heal, and provision for every meal.

Yes, there is pardon for every sin and the presence of God that dwells within. That is the experience of the ones God buys again. God redeems with justice and righteousness is the refrain. Thank you for redemption, Lord. Amen.

"We have been redeemed" is Zion's song,
sung by her repentant, righteous ones.

289

Sin Finds Out

But if you fail to keep your word, then you will have sinned against the Lord, and you may be sure that your sin will find you out.

NUMBERS 32:23 (NLT)

It is a natural principle of life that if we build with straw, the wind will show up and show us up. Similarly, the seeds we sow have an appointed day of harvest when they will show us up.

This truth Moses taught the people. He said, "Be sure your sins will find you out." This word of caution is still needed in our time, as the virtues of integrity and sincerity seem to be things of the past. We need to remember that our actions have consequences. Therefore, if we do not want to be found out by sin, do not let it come in. Amen.

Cleanse my heart and my mouth
so sin won't find me out.

290

The Lord Is

Lord, you are my strength and fortress,
my refuge in the day of trouble!
JEREMIAH 16:19 (NLT)

When Jeremiah found himself in distress as his nation faced impending invasion and subsequent destruction, he made the bold declaration, "The Lord is my strength, the Lord is my fortress, and the Lord is my refuge."

Though these words offer a glimpse of his peril, they also share his perspective of God's presence with him. He is assured of God's security, provision, and protection. So, next time you feel weak, draw from God's strength. When you are faced with foes, hide in him. And when you need to run away, run into him. Be safe. Amen.

God is your strength and fortress,
a safe refuge in the time of distress.

291

God Knows

But he knows the way that I take; when he has tested me, I will come forth as gold.

JOB 23:10 (NIV)

Life's journey is sometimes lonely and perilous. Like Robinson Crusoe, we are shipwrecked, alone and abandoned on no-man's-island. But God is not oblivious to our pain and misery. God is aware of the path we are taking, and he makes a personal choice to walk with us.

This awareness that God is with us changes our perspective. And so we understand the trial is only a test. And when it is over, and it will be over, we will be the victorious ones. Like pure gold that has been purified in the fire to reveal its true value and worth, we will come through victoriously. Thank you, Lord. Amen.

Let me be purified,
and God will be glorified.

292

Prayer Hearer

You who answer prayer, to you all people will come.

PSALM 65:2 (NIV)

It is like a breath of fresh air to make the astounding discovery that there is a God who hears prayer and all people can come to him! There are no distinctions based on class, gender, or creed. His ears are open to all those in need.

And whoever comes to him in faith, he gladly receives them. Today, you and I are invited to be part of the crew. Our names are on the list. So, let's go to Jesus, our lives to renew. God, I come to you. Amen.

God is the one who hears prayer.
Remember God is always near.

293

Full Understanding

"Behold, God is mighty, and does not despise any; he is mighty in strength of understanding."

JOB 36:5 (ESV)

God's character is impeccable, and his strength is unmatchable. Yet he takes notice of us, men and women, mere mortals. He despises none. Why does God, who is above and beyond human beings, take notice of them? I believe the answer lies both in his person and his purpose. God made mortals for a relationship with himself.

God is so awesome and so mighty that he is incapable of spurning others less than himself. We can be confident God will remain firm in his love toward us. We are forever under God's radar, and he will always give us his strength. Oh, may we realize we are never despised. Amen.

God of strength and understanding,
of our lives
you have full commanding.

294

Reward Will Come

"Keep your voice from weeping, and your eyes from tears,
for there is a reward for your work, declares the Lord."
JEREMIAH 31:16 (ESV)

Good people serve others out of the goodness of their hearts. Their service may not be appreciated, yet they serve. These people serve in obscurity, with anonymity, and without security. They are unknown and unrewarded by men but rewarded by God.

Jeremiah worked for the salvation of his people, and now it looked as if all was lost. He was disappointed and discouraged, but God spoke to him. "Stop weeping and dry up your tears!" As God said to Jeremiah, he says to us, "Dry your tears." Remember, when no one else sees, God does, and God will reward you for your work. Bless God! Amen.

We will keep working for the Lord;
all our labor he will reward.

295

Safe Sleep

In peace I will lie down and sleep, for you alone, O Lord will keep me safe.

PSALM 4:8 (NLT)

While living alone in a particular community, the news broke that a dangerous convict had escaped from prison. A neighbor discouraged me from staying in my home, fearing that I could be attacked. I affirmed that I was all right. Alone in the house after dark, however, I could not sleep.

As fear consumed me, I checked and rechecked doors and looked under the beds. Finally, I said to myself, "This is ridiculous. Help, Lord!" Then the Lord reminded me that he is the one who keeps me safe. So, I lay down in peace and slept. I thank you, Lord, for sweet, refreshing, restoring sleep. Amen.

It is God alone who keeps,
so lie down in peace and go to sleep.

296

God's People

The Lord was pleased to make you his own.

1 SAMUEL 12:22 (NIV)

God selected us to be his special people. He called us into a relationship with him and chose us to be his possession. It was his delight to do so. We are to be separated and sanctified for his glory. What does this separation mean?

First of all, we are not our own; we belong to God. Secondly, we must represent him on the earth and be conformed to the image of his Son. And finally, we must own his mandate and usher in his kingdom. God is delighted to choose us to participate with him. Let us also choose him. Remember, we are God's delight. Thank you, Lord. Amen.

I am precious in God's sight.
I am his chosen delight.

297

Holy Intercessor

He bore the sins of many and interceded for rebels.

ISAIAH 53:12 (NLT)

Every transgressor is doomed to die. We escape by God's righteous justice only because of Jesus's ministry of intercession. In intercession, Jesus goes between and interrupts the intention of the enemy. His going between also involves intercepting and halting the enemy's onslaught against us.

Jesus took this role upon himself when he went between the enemy and us by dying on the cross. There, he carried our sins. He accepted the judgment against us in satanic courts, and he paid the penalty. Now we can walk free. Hallelujah! Amen.

Friend, you are free.
Walk in your liberty.

298

The Lord Knows

The Lord knows the thoughts of man,
that they are but a breath.
PSALM 94:11 (ESV)

God inhabits eternity. He is aware of all our thoughts. He knows how we think, what we think, and why we think the way we think. In his scheme of things, our thoughts are merely a breath. It is God who gives us breath, and it is God who takes it away.

God is therefore not moved by our thoughts, however lofty they are. He knows they are perishable, and so are we. Let us submit our thoughts to God, who is from eternity to eternity. Lord, you rule and reign in our thoughts in our lives. Thank you. Amen.

God gives the very breath we take.
God knows our moments, asleep or awake.

299

God's Servants

He makes his messengers winds, his ministers a flaming fire.

PSALM 104:4 (ESV)

People are usually referred to as servants, but with God, everyone and everything is his servant. The wind is his messenger, and fire and flame are his ministers. Have you ever wondered how God sends the wind to make a message? And how do fire and flame obey his command? What about lightning and thunder? All are under his command. All do his bidding.

So, the next time you see lightning flashing or hear wind rustling, give praise. They are performing God's commands. Use us all as your messengers, Lord. Amen.

Lord, no one can be compared to you.
You are awesome in all you do.

300

Teach Us to Pray

"Lord, teach us to pray, just as John taught his disciples."

LUKE 11:1 (NLT)

Jesus lived and breathed a life of prayer. His entire persona was affected and directed by his prayer life. Prayer brought heaven's and earth's resources to his disposal. As Jesus emerged from one of his periods of prayer, the disciples expressed their desire to benefit from prayer as he did. They said to him, "Lord, teach us to pray."

The request was simple yet bold. Like the disciples, our requests to God for the things that benefit us and advance his kingdom should be asked with boldness. Lord, give us the desire to pray, and please teach us how. Amen.

Prayer opens our hearts
and in God's kingdom
gives us a part.

301

Public Confession

"I tell you, whoever publicly acknowledges me before others, the Son of Man will also acknowledge before the angels of God."

LUKE 12:8 (NIV)

Some people keep their relationship with Jesus a private affair. However, our relationship, although personal, is not private. Jesus is willing to acknowledge us before the angels in heaven when we acknowledge him publicly.

When we confess Jesus as Lord and Savior, we confess our dependence upon him and witness to what he has done and is doing in our lives. When we do not speak up for what is right, blend in with the culture, and keep silent about our faith, we fail to acknowledge Jesus as our Lord. If we own him, he owns us. Lord, we own you with every fiber of our being. Amen.

We acknowledge we belong, Lord.
We publicly own you as our God.

302

Holy Talk

The Lord said to Moses, "Speak to the entire assembly of Israel and say to them: 'Be holy because I, the Lord your God, am holy."

LEVITICUS 19:1–2 (NIV)

God speaks holiness and lives holiness. God is holiness. Because God is holy, it is natural for him to have the same desires for his children. To be holy is to be set apart for God's use. Personal holiness is the evidence of our relationship with a holy God.

God desires that we be holy in all aspects of our lives—holiness in our thinking, holiness in our talking, holiness in our eating, holiness in our working, holiness in our sleeping, and holiness in our playing. Yes, God desires holiness in our living. To live right is to live holy. Father, heal us and help us to live holy. Amen.

When we live holy,
God gets the glory.

303

Do It Freely

Heal the sick, raise the dead, cure those with leprosy, and cast out demons. Give as freely as you have received!

MATTHEW 10:8 (NLT)

Out of the goodness of his heart, God does good for us all the time. He heals and delivers. He provides and protects. God does not count the cost before he blesses us. Neither does he check the balance in his storehouse before he supplies the need. He simply lavishes us with his resources.

Since we are beneficiaries of his generosity, God expects us to reciprocate. We must share God's blessings with others. We must never get too attached to the tangibles and forget that there is more in God's storehouse. Remember, God is our source, and we are all tributaries. Let it flow freely. Amen.

Do not block the flow.
Let your generosity show!

304

I Am

And God said to Moses, "I am Yahweh—'the Lord.'"
EXODUS 6:2 (NLT)

God is the initiator of every covenant. He can be counted on to keep his word. God keeping God's word is a very important part of being God. God reminded Moses, "I am God, the Lord." That means that God cannot change and can be counted on as faithful.

So, when God says, "I am the Lord," he references the covenant that he made with his friend Abraham. It was proof to Moses that God can be trusted. Moses came to understand this truth that God is Provider, Sustainer, and Protector … whatever he needed God to be. Through adversity, perplexity, and prosperity, we too can trust God. Amen.

Holy God, almighty Lord,
is God who keeps his word.

305

Better Than Fowls

Consider the ravens: They do not sow or reap, they have no storeroom or barn, yet God feeds them.

LUKE 12:24 (NIV)

God is an amazing, awesome, and almighty. He manages the affairs of the universe, yet he pays attention to the intimate details that concern the welfare of the lower order of creation, such as fowls.

God provides for birds and bees. And if he ensures that they are fed and well cared for, how much more will he take care of you and me? Do you doubt that you are high on his agenda? There is no comparison. Your concerns are so covered. Thank you, Lord! Amen.

If the ravens get fed,
we will be supplied with daily bread.

306

More Room

"For now the Lord has made room for us,
and we shall be fruitful in the land."
GENESIS 26:22 (ESV)

God is for prosperity, productivity, and increase. He makes room for us and gives us the capacity to be fruitful. His excellence will not allow him to accept less from us. As God's children, productivity and prosperity should be evidenced in our lives.

The increase is God's desire and destiny for us. God's increase involves enlarged territories and extended borders. Since God has already provided the room, it is only a matter of time before we experience our prosperity. I believe we are already walking in it. In God, we do not get by; we flourish. Praise him! Amen.

Authority plus liberty
equals prosperity.

307

Give and Get

For if you forgive others their trespasses, your heavenly Father will also forgive you.
MATTHEW 6:14 (ESV)

If God forgives us when we forgive others, does it follow that if we do not forgive others, God does not forgive us? I believe it is implicit and explicit truth. It behooves us, my family, to forgive others so that we may be forgiven.

If we have not forgiven freely, there might be many prayers for forgiveness that God has not answered. I hope none of yours are included. Let us give forgiveness to others since we want to get forgiveness from God. Remember, there is no getting without giving. Lord, we forgive all those who have trespassed against us. Amen.

All who have hurt me, I release;
today I choose to have God's peace.

308

Let Go

"Go in to Pharaoh and say to him, 'Thus says the Lord, "Let my people go, that they may serve me."'"

EXODUS 8:1 (ESV)

The time had come for the Israelites to leave Egyptian slavery. To free them, God first tried diplomacy. "Tell Pharaoh, 'Let my people go.'" Pharaoh thought he had too much to lose if he let the people go. So he allowed pride and the stubbornness of his heart to reject God's diplomacy.

Pharaoh's actions cost him many things, including the lives of the firstborns of Egypt. What instructions to let go have you been given? Let go! If you do not respond to God's love, you will have to respond to God's power. Make us yielded to your love, Lord. Amen.

Let go and yield;
God will be your shield.

309

Lose to Gain

Whoever finds their life will lose it, and whoever loses their life for my sake will find it.

MATTHEW 10:39 (NIV)

One person's loss is usually another person's gain. It is not usual that your loss is your gain. With Christ, however, this is the norm; when you lose, you gain.

Authentic living requires that we embrace Christ and the values of his kingdom. This may mean that we lose our status and position before others. We must be prepared to give up what we desire for what Christ desires. We lose to gain. Christ offers us a new and better way. Lord, we give up our lives. May we find it in you. Amen.

Lord, this is a glorious new day.
Lead us in your newfound way.

310

Command Conscious

"Even if Balak gave me all the silver and gold in his palace, I could not do anything great or small to go beyond the command of the Lord my God."

NUMBERS 22:18 (NIV)

We are tempted to do what others tell us because of the potential benefits we may derive from doing so. King Balak promised Balaam many things if he would curse the Israelite people. Balaam admitted that he could not curse them beyond God's command to do so.

We, too, will experience temptations to do wrong. We must be conscious of God's command and do all within our power to obey. The next time you are tempted, think about God's command. Lord, we put all things in your hands. Help us not to go beyond your command. Amen.

We move only to God's Word.
We do nothing until his voice is heard.

311

So Satisfied

They all ate and were satisfied, and the disciples picked up twelve basketfuls of broken pieces that were left over.

LUKE 9:17 (NIV)

When last did you experience the emotion of being satisfied after having a meal? As a child, that satisfied feeling was accompanied by the words "Ma belly full." It was a good feeling.

Jesus fed the disciples and the crowd with fives loaves and two fishes. They were so satisfied that they had twelve baskets of broken fragments to spare. This suggests that when God blesses, he always gives more than enough to meet our needs. This God of more than enough is willing to satisfy our deepest longings. Let us tell him about the needs of our hearts. Lord, feed us. Amen.

We have deep desires
and longings inside.
Lord, feed us until we are satisfied.

312

When God Is with You

But the Lord was with Joseph and showed him steadfast love and gave him favor in the sight of the keeper of the prison.
GENESIS 39:21 (ESV)

When God is in our lives, it shows. We have the power to magnetize kindness and favor, and people who come into contact with us are willing to bless us.

As a prisoner and a slave, Joseph could have simply given up, but he did each task with diligence and care. Yes, he was wrongfully mistreated, but Joseph maintained a good attitude and practiced a good work ethic. The warden admired Joseph's dedication to duty and promoted him to the rank of prison administrator. When the Lord is with us, he opens every door before us. Thank you, Lord. Amen.

When God is with us, we know honor.
When God is with us, we walk in favor.

313

Loosed

"Woman, you are freed from your disability."
LUKE 13:12 (ESV)

The religious leaders of Jesus's day considered healing as the practice of one's profession. As such, healing was work and if practiced on the Sabbath would be considered a violation of the Sabbath.

Jesus healed a woman on the Sabbath. He broke religious tradition and carried out the law of compassion. He loosed this crippled woman from her sins, her fears, her past. What do you need to be loosed from? Jesus is right by your side. He pronounces these words to you: "Be loosed!" Thank you, Jesus, for loosing us from everything that keeps us bound and infirm. Amen.

Sickness and disease cannot stand
when Jesus stretches out his healing hand.

314

Big Wish

"I wish that all the Lord's people were prophets and that the Lord would put his Spirit on them!"

NUMBERS 11:29 (NIV)

Aaron and Miriam thought that Moses was full of himself when he used his God-given gift in the practice of ministry. They accused him of behaving as if he were the only prophet God could use. Moses replied, "I wish that all God's people were prophets." Moses wanted everyone to have what he had.

God gives gifts to every one of us. When these gifts are displayed in others, there is no need to become jealous. Just ask God to use you mightily, and he will. He will give you the ability, but you must match it with your availability. Lord, I am available. Amen.

Lord, with sincerity and humility
we announce our availability.

315

Success Plan

Commit to the Lord whatever you do, and
he will establish your plans.
PROVERBS 16:3 (NIV)

Commitment to God is critical for success in life. Commitment involves ensuring that our plans give glory to God and not to ourselves. It also involves exerting effort to execute the plan. More importantly, commitment requires that we relinquish control of what we do to God.

When we commit to the Lord, we understand that we are but instruments in the Lord's hand. We are ready to be used anywhere, anytime, anyway. We say, "Lord, whatever we do, let it bring honor to you." Amen.

Successful life plans
are those placed in God's hands.

316

Can't Lose

"And whoever gives one of these little ones even a cup of cold water because he is a disciple, truly, I say to you, he will by no means lose his reward."

MATTHEW 10:42 (ESV)

We can never lose with Jesus because God pays his bills on time. Even a cup of cold water given on his behalf guarantees a payment. Giving to others makes God indebted to us, and thus he is obligated to bless us. We might think a cup of cold water is nothing, but for God, it is everything.

God knows how we contribute to building his kingdom and honoring his name. Other people may not see or acknowledge our efforts, but God does, and he will reward us. We do not serve for the payment, but when it comes, we give thanks. Thank you, Lord. Amen.

We can never lose
when to serve God we choose.

317

Chosen Instrument

But the Lord said to him, "Go, for he is a chosen instrument of mine to carry my name before the Gentiles and kings and the children of Israel."

ACTS 9:15 (ESV)

We easily write off others because of their past, making the determination they are not worthy of God's use. The apostle Paul was first a persecutor of the church. Then he met Jesus, the Christ, and became a changed man. How possible was it for the persecutor to become the proclaimer?

Ananias knew of Saul's past and questioned Saul's sincerity. God assured him, "He is my chosen instrument." Ananias ministered to Saul and enabled Saul to serve better. We must remember everyone is a potential instrument. Our mission is to help tune them. Help us to help, Lord. Amen.

Let us be encouragers,
meeting the needs of brothers and sisters.

318

Faith on Power

I did this so you would trust not in human wisdom but in the power of God.

1 CORINTHIANS 2:5 (NLT)

The apostle Paul was a brilliant scholar who could have used his intellectual wit to persuade people about God. Instead, he used simple words and simple faith and depended on the Holy Spirit to guide him. Paul's wisdom could not save, but God, who he preached, the God who met people at their point of need, did.

When Paul trusted God, he witnessed God's demonstrable power working on his behalf. He convinced others that the best place to rest their faith was the power of God. I agree. We rest our faith in you, Lord. Amen.

Faith grows and towers
when it rests on God's power.

319

More Blessed

Jesus replied, "But even more blessed are all who hear the word of God and put it into practice."
LUKE 11:28 (NLT)

In Jesus's day, a man's worth was measured by the wealth of his ancestral family, and a woman's worth was measured by the number of sons she had. Those variables determined whether a person was blessed or not.

Jesus established a new order, a new measure. He taught that children and good family names do not determine a person's blessedness, but hearing and obeying God's Word does. Jesus made it clear that position, power, and prestige are no longer the indicators of true blessedness, but obeying God's Word is. So, how blessed are you? Let us obey and be blessed. Give us grace, Lord. Amen.

More blessed to hear and obey,
be more blessed day by day.

320

Build Your Altar

And there he built an altar and called the place El-bethel, because there God had revealed himself to him when he fled from his brother.

GENESIS 35:7 (ESV)

Building an altar is a deliberate decision to keep a memorial. It is a personal reminder and a way of calling others to witness the great things that God has done in you. It is also an invitation to God to come to you.

Jacob remembered running like a fugitive from his brother Esau. He had done him wrong and justly deserved his fury, but God intervened and saved Jacob's life. God still intervenes in our lives to save us from destructive habits and lifestyles. Let us build an altar and let God's intervention be the defining moment in our lives. I lay myself at your altar, Lord. Amen.

Let us build an altar
and our prayers and thanksgiving offer.

321

Joy, Joy

"Just so, I tell you, there is joy before the angels of God over one sinner who repents."

LUKE 15:10 (ESV)

God is a loving parent who desires to have meaningful relationships with his children. Sin and rebellion, however, interrupt that relationship, injure us, and grieve God. When we repent, the broken relationship is restored, and heaven rejoices.

The repentant sinner brings God the greatest joy. The question for every one of us to answer is, What do you bring to God's heart? Joy or sadness? Let us choose joy. The joy of sin forgiven is the real joy of heaven. Lord, we repent. Amen.

Make it your life's employ
to give God some joy!

322

None Other

"Salvation is found in no one else, for there is no other name under heaven given to mankind by which we must be saved."

ACTS 4:12 (NIV)

No other means of salvation, no other means of deliverance and restoration? This is a very serious claim that Jesus made and fulfilled. He came to earth as God's only Son and offered himself as the sacrifice for our sins.

When we trust in that name to have our sins forgiven, our past is forgotten, and we are made righteous before God. Our needs are provided, and our lives are protected. In that name alone, every impossible situation becomes possible. What a name! Yes, there is no other name! Hallelujah!

God's Most High and holy name,
what an honor to proclaim.

323

Boaster

Therefore, as it is written: "Let the one who boasts boast in the Lord."
1 CORINTHIANS 1:31 (NIV)

Human beings tend to boast. We boast of the possessions we own and the positions we hold. We boast of the power we have and the people we helped to save. We boast of people's opinions of us and the human accolades they give to us.

It is sobering to note, however, that our achievements in life cannot secure a new life in Jesus Christ; only the blood of Jesus can. We can do nothing to earn Christ's love. He gives it to us as a free gift. If we boast, therefore, let our boasting be about the Lord who gives us all things. We are boasters for you, Lord. Amen.

From coast to coast,
use your breath God's love to boast.

324

Love's Desire

This is the message you have heard from the beginning: We should love one another.

1 JOHN 3:11 (NLT)

Love is a deep desire to see the greatest good for the other. How do we get such a desire? Cultivate it. Sow a seed of kindness; water it with grace; remove the weeds with patience; fertilize it with forgiveness; watch it grow with compassion; and harvest it in peace.

Remember, God has shed abroad his love in your heart. The seed of love is already planted in you. This gives you the capacity to love as Christ loves. Thank you, Lord, for your help. We only need to allow it to grow. Amen.

Nurture seeds of love every day.
Know great things will come your way.

325

When Fear Meets Love

Such love has no fear because perfect love expels all fear. If we are afraid, it is for fear of punishment, and this shows that we have not fully experienced his perfect love.

1 JOHN 4:18 (NLT)

God predetermined that the judgment for sin is death. The possibility of death, however, carries great fear. The good news is God also made provision for life. New life is given through the death of his Son, Jesus Christ.

If we accept this provision, this sacrifice, there is no need to fear. Our fear will always be swallowed up in God's perfect love. Lord, we appreciate your love and thank you for removing our fear. Amen.

Because God is love and God is near,
God's perfect love drives out our fear.

326

Genuine Love

We love because he first loved us.

1 JOHN 4:19 (ESV)

Genuine love is manifested when the lover gives love without any expectation of receiving back the love given. The lover continues to love until the one who is loved responds to the lover with the love given.

Genuine love asks no payback. Neither does it hold back when it is not returned. It continues to love until the one loved is moved by the love received. God loves us until we became capable of loving him. O first lover of our souls, we thank you for your unconditional love. Amen.

God, our hearts respond to you.
Your love is genuine and true.

327

In Pursuit of Peace

Let him turn away from evil and do good;
let him seek peace and pursue it.
1 PETER 3:11 (ESV)

Peace! Peace! Nothing is broken! Everything is whole!
There is a feeling of wellness deep in the soul.
In all my relationships, I work for the good, treating other persons the way I should.
Of course, there are moments when we misunderstand
and fight each other rather than lend a helping hand.
Then we remember, from greatest to least,
God has commanded us to pursue peace.
With determined effort, Lord, we go after peace. Amen.

When we pursue peace,
all our striving and trouble will cease.

328

Moved by Our Cry

And will not God bring about justice for his chosen ones, who cry out to him day and night?
LUKE 18:7 (NIV)

God is protective of those who have no helper. He takes the side of the oppressed who is bereft of justice. He listens to their cry. When they bring a matter before him for adjudication, God as the supreme judge has no other choice but to act on behalf of justice.

Because God can discern the thoughts and intentions of our hearts, he can judge with fairness. We can rest assured that God will act swiftly. He will act on our behalf. Remember, his heart is touched by the cry of his own. Justice shall be served! We thank you, Lord.

Thank you, Lord, for our cry moves you.
We wait with patience for what you will do.

329

Dead and Alive

In the same way, count yourselves dead to sin but alive to God in Christ Jesus.

ROMANS 6:11 (NIV)

It is quite an amazing feat to be dead and alive at the same time. We can be dead to sin but alive to God. This means that we must regard our old nature as no longer responsive to sin. It may tempt us, but we are under no obligation to respond. What makes this possible?

Our union to Christ makes us alive in him. This gives us the power to resist temptation and be dead to sin. Through Jesus, we have access to a sin-ignore button. We need to press it! It works! Lord, let me be dead to sin and alive to you only. Amen.

Friend, make the death of sin sure.
Be alive to Jesus even more.

330

With You

"I am the God of your father Abra-ham. Do not be afraid, for I am with you; I will bless you and will increase the number of your descendants for the sake of my servant Abraham."

GENESIS 26:24 (NIV)

Fear is a common human experience. I believe all of us can admit to being afraid. When others stand by us in a difficult situation, fear is lessened, and we tend to feel secure.

God has assured us of his persistent presence in our lives. No matter what the circumstances are, he will be with us and will provide security. We have no reason to fear. God also promises blessings in abundance and the preservation of our posterity. We thank you, Lord, for your presence with us. Amen.

God is present with me.
God preserves my posterity.

331

Alive

But God, being rich in mercy, because of the great love with which he loved us, even when we were dead in our trespasses, made us alive together with Christ.

EPHESIANS 2:4–5 (ESV)

God is Creator, Owner, and Sustainer of the universe. He is awesome and excellent in all his ways. He is rich in every resource known and unknown. By any stretch of the imagination, God is loaded.

Of all the resources that God owns, God uses mercy to give us life in Christ. Mercy is God's decision not to give us what we justly deserve. Instead, God gives us what we need to live. We need his mercy. Mercy, Lord! Have mercy on us, Lord. Have mercy. Amen.

We are made alive by mercy.
To God be the glory.

332

All Healed

The people also gathered from the towns around Jerusalem, bringing the sick and those afflicted with unclean spirits, and they were all healed.

ACTS 5:16 (ESV)

That must have been a spectacular sight to see the sick coming from all around and being healed. This only attests to the awesomeness of the power of God at work through Jesus Christ to heal and save.

God's power is still available to us, even this minute. Right where you are, and whatever your troubles and turmoil, God's healing power is available to you. Take this moment and inhale his peace to heal every torment in your soul. Breathe. You are whole. Amen.

God gives his blood as the seal.
All our sickness and diseases he heals.

333

Love Does Not Condemn

For God did not send his Son into the world
to condemn the world through him.
JOHN 3:17 (NIV)

When God looked at our brokenness, rebellion, sin, and shame and made his judgment, He gave the verdict: guilty. We were guilty, and our sentence was death. Yet God's love was greater than our death sentence. God's love compelled him to send Jesus to offer us salvation.

Jesus did not condemn us. He became our sin and gave us his righteousness. He assumed our guilt and allowed us to walk free. Yes, Jesus gave his life so we could have liberty. Advocate and Helper, accept our gratefulness today. Amen.

We are no longer condemned; we are free!
What love!
What liberty!

334

Just Do

"Do whatever he tells you."

JOHN 2:5 (NIV)

Jesus was at a wedding in Cana where they ran out of wine, the key ingredient in the celebration. This situation left the family exposed to ridicule. With no convenience store nearby and no money to purchase the wine, the family was in a quandary.

Mary, Jesus's mother, makes him aware of the potentially embarrassing family situation. She tells the servants, "Whatever he says, just do." They obeyed and got wine to remedy the situation. Maybe you have a situation. Mary's words of wisdom are for you: "What he says, just do." Help us to obey you, Lord. Amen.

No need to rationalize;
simply obey with faith's eyes.

335

When Little Is Much

"There is a boy here who has five barley loaves and two fish, but what are they for so many?"

JOHN 6:9 (ESV)

There is always so much to do with so little to go around. With the most liberal stretch of the imagination, we still ask, "How will these few serve so many?" In the natural order, it could never be enough. The miracle in little becoming much, however, lies in the breaking.

You break once and get two; you break twice and get four; break the third time and get sixteen, you break the fourth time and get thirty-two. Keep breaking until you reach infinity. By the time breaking is completed, everyone will have received more than enough. Keep breaking. Help us, Lord. Amen.

Little will become much
when submitted to God's master touch.

336

Walk Worthily

We exhorted each one of you and encouraged you and charged you to walk in a manner worthy of God, who calls you into his own kingdom and glory.

1 THESSALONIANS 2:12 (ESV)

Walking worthily before God is to acknowledge God as God. It is to live in a way that pleases God and proclaim him to the world. Parents are pleased with children who display exemplary attitudes, behavior, and character. These children are obedient, and the parents are proud to call them their own.

We must be obedient to our heavenly Father and imitate him in our conduct and character. By so doing, we walk worthily of him. Let's give our Father glory and walk worthily. Amen.

Let us walk *worthily*,
and God will get the glory.

337

Time of Favor

"In the time of my favor I heard you, and in the day of salvation I helped you." I tell you, now is the time of God's favor, now is the day of salvation.

2 CORINTHIANS 6:2 (NIV)

God wants us to know his salvation. He is aware of our needs and knows where we are stranded. In his time of favor, he heard us, and at the opportune time, when we need him most, he appears in response to our cries and helps us. God shows up with his salvific actions and addresses every debilitating and tormenting situation.

Ah, God! How incredibly awesome you are! Just when we need you most, you are there and on time. You heard our cries for help and met our needs. Hallelujah! Amen.

God, we thank you for hearing
and for your loving acts of saving.

338

Sons through Faith

So in Christ Jesus, you are all children of God through faith.

GALATIANS 3:26 (NIV)

Not many of us can claim noble birth. Many of us were born in obscurity and struggled to find our identity. Even in adult life, many of us never fulfill our destiny because we remain stuck in the cocoon of immaturity. Our low self-esteem hinders our ability to see ourselves as children of God and royalty.

Through faith in Christ Jesus, our identity is changed; we become sons and daughters of God. Our DNA is reconfigured. We are recalibrated and recreated. That is nobility. Hallelujah!

Christ Jesus, you are the one.
Through you, we are God's daughters and sons.

339

Sin Talks

If we confess our sins, he is faithful and just to forgive us our sins and to cleanse us from all unrighteousness.

1 JOHN 1:9 (ESV)

Sin is missing the mark and choosing to walk in rebellion rather than in obedience. It is creating new paths for our walking feet rather than being with God on Grace Street. We have all been soiled by the ruble on that path before, but today is confessing day.

Confessing our sins is our acknowledging that we have offended and dishonored God. It restores our right relationship with God by giving us the blessing of God's forgiveness. Thank you for forgiveness, Lord. Amen.

Our sins we will confess.
We are healed and blessed.

340

Greater Is He That Is in Me

For he who is in you is greater than he who is in the world.

1 JOHN 4:4 (ESV)

The world is full of greatness: great people, ideas, inventions, and innovations. Sadly, we must acknowledge there is also great wickedness through a sponsor and promoter of evil, Satan.

But that is not the end of the story. For God is greater than every power, and God lives within us. We are not lacking the power to overcome, for the power resides on the inside of us, and this power is greater than any power in the world. Great God, we thank you for depositing greatness in us. Amen.

In us live the Father, Spirit, and Son,
so we know for sure we will overcome.

341

Commander, Come

"Neither one," he replied. "I am the commander of the Lord's army."
JOSHUA 5:14 (NLT)

We are soldiers in God's army, fighting the enemy: Satan, his cohorts, and the host of darkness. There are times when the engagement of the enemy is frightening. We appear to be outnumbered, and defeat seems sure, but then reinforcements always appear.

God's angel showed up in Joshua's time of battle: "I have come now as commander of the armies of the Lord." This is a gentle, powerful, and effective reminder that the battle is not ours but the Lord's. So, gird your loins, soldier. Remain in place, knowing you are anchored with God's grace. Thank you for backup, Lord. Amen.

The *Captain* of the Lord's host
is armed, already standing at his post.

342

Nonsnatchable

For my, Father has given them to me, and he is more powerful than anyone else. No one can snatch them from the Father's hand.

JOHN 10:29 (NLT)

We have heard of purse snatchers, body snatchers, identity snatchers—in fact, all kinds of snatchers. These are people who watch your movements and look for vulnerable moments to pounce on you, robbing you of your valuables—purse, children, gold, and other precious tangibles.

In God's hand, we are not snatchable. We may be tempted to believe that we are exposed and powerless against the enemy but hear the truth: no one can or will ever be able to snatch us out of his hand. So, rest there, my friend. He will hold us safely to the end. Amen.

In God's enfolding arms,
we are kept safe from all harm.

343

Refreshing

Repent, then, and turn to God, so that your sins may be wiped out, that times of refreshing may come from the Lord.

ACTS 3:19 (NIV)

Sin and rebellion are hard taskmasters. They cost more than we can afford to pay, they carry us further than we intended to stray, and they confuse our minds and make us lose our way. God offers us this invitation: repent and turn to God.

When we do, God forgives our sins and blots out every trace of them. He grants us renewal and restoration. I don't know about you, but I affirm my need for restoration and renewal. I am returning. Will you join me? We are coming, Lord. Amen.

Let's repent and return.
Let God's fire in us burn.

344

Free to Serve

For you were called to freedom, brothers. Only do not use your freedom as an opportunity for the flesh, but through love serve one another.

GALATIANS 5:13 (ESV)

We become enslaved to unwholesome habits more easily than we think. Ask the drug addict or the alcoholic. They will concur. Christ knew that sin had the power to enslave, so he came to rescue us from sin's grasp.

Christ has called us into freedom. Freedom is not the right to do as we choose but the willingness to use our power responsibly. With freedom also comes the responsibility to serve one another in love. Let us use our freedom to serve. Amen.

I serve because I am free.
Lord, increase your service in me.

345

Be Strong

Finally, be strong in the Lord and the strength of his might.
EPHESIANS 6:10 (ESV)

Each of us has been endowed with personal power. We choose what to wear, what to eat, who to love, and who not to love. Each action is an expression of our power. It is important to understand that even though we have power, human power is exhaustive and cannot be relied upon.

Reliable, inexhaustible power comes from God. God's power is limitless, boundless, and available to us. Let us be strong with the Lord's power that never fails, never ends, and can never be overcome. In him, we can be strong. Praise Jah!

Remember God's power is unshakable
and his kingdom unstoppable.

346

Continue

And now, just as you accepted Christ Jesus as your Lord, you must continue to follow him.
COLOSSIANS 2:6 (NLT)

It is easier to begin than to continue. Continuing is difficult and demands a certain level of discipline, which requires time and effort to cultivate. It involves getting past the distractions that line the road and navigating various bends and detours. There are the valleys of discouragement that one must overcome. No wonder so many people cease to continue.

As people of faith, we must continue our walk with God. The roots of our relationship must go deep enough to anchor us to the unending supply of Christ's love, mercy, and grace. So then continue. Continue to live in Christ. Lord, we need your help! Amen.

Let's continue.
Our faith we will renew.

347

Full Armor

Put on all of God's armor so that you will be able to stand firm against all strategies of the devil.

EPHESIANS 6:11 (NLT)

In the Christian life, we encounter powerful forces that impede our walk. These forces of darkness have the potential to damage, debilitate, and even destroy us. Is there any defense for us? Of course! There is the full armor of God with which we must clothe ourselves.

God's armor offers a defense that the enemy cannot penetrate. The soldier who puts on his helmet with no shield knows he is exposed. The only solution is full armor. When we put on the full armor, we stand in the shade of God's good hand. Show us how to gear up each day, Lord. Amen.

Put on the full armor
and walk in God's protective power.

348

Love Heals

"I will heal their waywardness and love them freely,
for my anger has turned away from them."
HOSEA 14:4 (NIV)

Every human being has the propensity for waywardness—the tendency to drift or turn away and backslide. How many times have we exhibited this tendency?

God is aware of our weaknesses and waywardness. Our rebellion causes deep pain for God and shows itself as God's anger. What is God's response to his anger? He decides to heal us. Punishment does not cure us; only his love can. God loves us freely, without reserve and measure. Oh, God, wrap us in this love. Hide the proclivities of our flesh. Amen.

The love heals our waywardness.
He covers us. What graciousness.

349

No Complaining

Do everything without grumbling or arguing.
PHILIPPIANS 2:14 (NIV)

Complaining, fussing, and arguing are like fingers of the same glove—inseparable. To complain is to express discontent and dissatisfaction and not in a straightforward but sullen manner. The motive is never to seek a solution but to cast aspersions, make personal attacks, and shame the individual who is deemed the source of the trouble.

The effect of complaining is deadly, and people of faith should never give room to this spirit. Complaining tears down rather than builds God's kingdom. People of God, we must not be complainers. Today we chose not to complain, Lord. Amen.

Those who murmur or complain,
God's kingdom they will not gain.

350

Content

I have learned the secret of being content in any and every situation, whether well fed or hungry, whether living in plenty or want.

PHILIPPIANS 4:12 (NIV)

Growing up, my parents always said, "Learn to have a contented mind and be satisfied with what you have." A contented person is grateful for what he or she has, is not envious, does not compete, and does not beg, borrow, or steal from others.

Paul was content because he saw things from God's perspective and concentrated on fulfilling God's purpose. Sometimes resources were scarce and he faced opposition, but Paul remained focused and did God's will. We, too, should be content and give thanks. Help us, Lord. Amen.

Be content with great or small.
Be focused on fulfilling God's call!

351

Grace

May the grace of the Lord Jesus Christ be with your spirit.
PHILIPPIANS 4:23 (NLT)

Grace! Grace! Grace! Wonderful, marvelous, undeserved, unmerited, and unmatched favor from God is ours. Grace is God coming to walk alongside us where we are stuck and unable to move. Grace is God coming to meet us at our point of need.

Grace is not an empty excuse for us to exist in a state of sin but the enabling power of God, which empowers us to say goodbye to a life of sin. Grace is the entry into an eternal relationship with God through Jesus Christ. Where would you be without grace? I know where I would be: dead. Thank you, God, for grace. Amen.

When grace fills our spirits,
eternal life we will inherit.

352

God with Men

"Behold, the dwelling place of God is with man."
REVELATION 21:3 (ESV)

God's dwelling place is with humanity. Hallelujah! God is with us, God is in us, and God is for us. How is it possible that the divine desires to abide with and keep company with mortals? It sounds unbelievable, yet it is true; the Almighty is present to us and abides with us.

Why does God desire this close affinity with humanity? Here is the reason: we belong to him, and he belongs to us. He is our God. Incredibly amazing! God shall dwell with us at our place of abode. God will walk with us and lighten our load. Thank you, Lord. Amen.

God is with you, his precious child.
To him be forever reconciled.

353

Wiped Tears

He will wipe away every tear from their eyes.
REVELATION 21:4 (ESV)

We can recall our tears when we were in deep distress,
tears of anguish we did not know how to address.
The tears were heavy, we must confess,
filled with pain, anger, and bitterness.
But God wipes the tears from our eyes today.
No more death or sorrow shall come our way.
God fills the darkness with his bright ray,
and the former things pass away.
We present our tears to you, Lord. Thank you for wiping them. Amen.

No matter what you are
going through, my friend,
God has the last word;
it is not the end.

354

Born in Hope

All praise to God, the Father of our Lord Jesus Christ.
It is by his great mercy that we have been born again
because God raised Jesus Christ from the dead.

1 PETER1:3 (NLT)

Sometimes we face situations that bring us to the end of ourselves and leave us feeling helpless. But praise God, he shows up with mercy. Mercy is Jesus restoring us, renewing us, and giving us eternal life. Mercy is Jesus paying the price for our sins.

Jesus is sufficient for every situation. For that habit you are desirous of breaking, for that spirit you have tried shaking, and for that condition with which you have difficulty coping, there is hope. We can have hope because Jesus has mercy. Amen.

Born again through God's great mercy,
raised from death, we walk in victory.

355

War and Win

Dear friends, I urge you, as foreigners and exiles, to abstain from sinful desires, which wage war against your soul.

1 PETER 2:11 (NIV)

Sometimes we create war when we practice attitudes and behaviors that appeal to our flesh. We know they are not the best and that they hinder rather than help our Christian walk, yet we embrace them.

Here is the challenge: let them go! Keep away from them. Yes, walk away from sinful desires and pleasures. Ahh! I hear a sigh. It is not so easy! I agree. Here is the deal: you leave them, and they will leave you. Lord, give us the courage to leave them behind. Amen.

Take offensive action.
Rid ourselves of lustful passion.

356

Zip It

When they hurled their insults at him, he did not retaliate; when he suffered, he made no threats. Instead, he entrusted himself to him who judges justly.

1 PETER 2:23 (NIV)

Jesus was accused, abused, and misused. He did not retaliate. He did not seek revenge. He committed it to God, the only one who judges righteously.

When we are accused wrongfully, we experience a myriad of emotions and feel the need to avenge ourselves. Yet we see Jesus, who did not lash back at his accusers but simply kept quiet. He zipped his mouth and left the issue to God. We should try Jesus's approach sometimes. God will work it out. Help us to trust you, Lord. Amen.

We don't need to answer people.
Leave the situation for God to handle.

357

Tamed Lions

My God sent his angel to shut the lions' mouths so that they would not hurt me, for I have been found innocent.

DANIEL 6:22 (NLT)

God permits his servants to undertake dangerous assignments that may lead us into the lions' den. We can rest assured that there God will tame the lions' mouths. The truth is we are untouchable.

We ought to remember that until and unless God gives the command to touch us, no one can. When we trust God, he gives immeasurable peace. We can rely on God's power to deliver us. If God delivered Daniel, God will deliver us. Trust him. Give more capacity to trust, Lord. Amen.

If divine assignment leads you
to the den of lions,
you can count on protection
from the God of Zion.

358

Returned

Once you were like sheep who wandered away. But now you have turned to your Shepherd, the Guardian of your souls.

1 PETER 2:25 (NLT)

Sheep exhibit a tendency to stray. They are lured by the green grass beyond the horizon and inch their way there, ignoring the dangers lurking in the path. Many times, they are oblivious to the danger, as they see only the green grass.

Human beings, like sheep, often stray from the good path. Our straying invites danger, destruction, disaster, and even death. Today, however, is Returning Day. We choose to return to the Shepherd and Guardian of our souls, who will nourish and nurture us. Give us the desire to return to you, Lord. We are coming home. Amen.

Shepherd of our souls, refresh and bless.
We return to feed on your faithfulness.

359

Christian Characteristics

Finally, all of you, have unity of mind, sympathy, brotherly love, a tender heart, and a humble mind.

1 PETER 3:8 (ESV)

A Christian mindset speaks of a mind infused with Christian values and virtues. Honesty, integrity, a willingness to work with others, sensitivity to the struggles that others face, the capacity to love deeply, a willingness to share your resources without grudges, and the capacity to rejoice and celebrate others—these are Christian characteristics.

When we determinedly and diligently develop these characteristics, we become an indestructible force for God and good. God, help us so to be. Amen.

Grow in grace and goodness.
Build a character of greatness.

360

The Sinner's Advocate

If anyone does sin, we have an advocate with the Father, Jesus Christ the righteous.

1 JOHN 2:1 (ESV)

What a privilege available to all sinners. We can employ the legal services of an advocate, Jesus Christ the Righteous. He knows the judge personally. And he paid our legal fees, including the fine that the judge demanded we must pay.

Jesus also bore the sentence of our confinement; therefore, the judge cannot deny him. He took our sentence of death, so now we walk free. That calls for a loud and exuberant shout! Hallelujah!

Jesus was condemned; we walk free.
Jesus paid the price of forgiveness; we live in victory.

361

Love and Light

Anyone who loves their brother and sister lives in the light, and there is nothing in them to make them stumble.

1 JOHN 2:10 (NIV)

I have met people who claimed they were enlightened, but their souls were full of bitterness, resentment, and hate. They kept a record of all the wrongs that were done to them and offered that as a reason why they could not love. What a contradiction! Light only dwells where love is. Or, expressed another way, where love is, there is light.

If you are experiencing a power outage, I urge you to take an inventory of your soul and see what is stored there. If you are low on love, chances are you are low on light. Lord, free us to love one another. Amen.

If love is hidden from your sight,
you are not walking in the light.

362

Sons

Dear friends, now we are children of God, and what we will have not yet been made known. But we know that when Christ appears, we shall be like him, for we shall see him as he is.

1 JOHN 3:2 (NIV)

That God could have children is a wonder to me, and that I am one of them is a double mystery. As God's child and heir, I know I have some entitlements that include both rights and responsibilities.

I have access to God and can seek his face. I can be like God, exercising his grace. All his resources are available to me anytime and anyplace. Amazingly, I am God's child, and yes, his kindness I can trace. Help me, Lord, to see your face and be fully like you. Amen.

Children of God, we are not ordinary.
We bear the image of the heavenly.

363

Keep Calm

Do not be quickly provoked in your spirit,
for anger resides in the lap of fools.
ECCLESIASTES 7:9 (NIV)

Some people are easily angered, and it takes real effort to keep their tempers under control. At the least offense, they explode in anger. They make foolish choices, uttering angry words that they later regret. It is customary then for such a person to say, "He or she made me so angry."

The truth is we have control of our spirits, and we determine whether we will allow ourselves to become provoked. Let us learn valuable lessons and keep our spirits calm and under our control. Help us, Lord. Amen.

The cover of God's balm
helps us keep our spirits calm.

364

Save Me

But when he saw the wind, he was afraid, and beginning to sink he cried out, "Lord, save me."
MATTHEW 14:30 (ESV)

Peter started with good intentions. Having recognized Jesus in the storm, he desired to go to him. But then his faith faltered in his attempt to exercise it. He cried out to Jesus, "Lord, save me!"

Perhaps there are things you started believing, ministries you started doing, but your faith faltered during your exercising. Remember this: faltering is not failing. Do like Peter and cry out to Jesus, "Help me!" He will reach out to you. Whenever we find our faith faltering, we need to remember we are not failing. Jesus is reaching to save us. Reach Jesus. Amen.

Our faltering and failing
give Jesus the opportunity
for reaching and saving.

365

Never Forsaken

For Israel and Judah have not been forsaken by their God, the Lord of hosts, but the land of the Chaldeans is full of guilt.

JEREMIAH 51:5 (ESV)

When people of faith sin and later experience difficulties, they wrongly conclude that God has forsaken them. But let me assure us that God does not forsake us when we sin.

We experience distance in our relationship because of the guilt we feel when our consciences convict us of the wrong. Jeremiah declared that though the people were guilty of the wrong, they would not be forsaken by God. Maybe you have done wrong, but God will not turn his back on you. Turn your face to him and repent. He will hold you fast to him. Help us to turn, Lord. Amen.

God sits on his holy throne.
He will not forsake his own.

366

Glory Forever

Now all glory to God our Father forever and ever! Amen.

—PHILIPPIANS 4:20 (NLT)

Glory, honor, dominion, and power belong to God. As the Creator of the ends of the earth and as Redeemer of our lives, he has earned this right to be worshipped and adored.

To worship is to show love and adoration. In worship, we assess God's worth and value to us. We determine what he means to us, and we express that to him. What is your assessment of God? What is God's worth to you? He is worth everything. So give God the glory forever and ever! Amen!

God is high and holy.
Forever, God deserves the glory.

Permissions

Endorsement

These 366 devotional verses and messages are refreshing, informative, inspiring, and rich.

I fully endorse this publication, which shall be of significant benefit for believers and convincing biblical evidence that is capable of convincing the unbeliever to believe.

—Bishop Dr. Conrad Spencer Ep. Fr

About the Author

Denise Smith-Lewis invited the Lord Jesus Christ into her life in her teen years. The experience confirmed her identity as God's daughter. She is Antiguan and Barbudan by birth and grew up in Antigua with her parents and siblings. The home was a place of missions where the hungry were fed and the homeless were brought in for shelter.

Denise discovered her passion for service then and has been in the pastoral ministry for twenty-eight years. She has served in her native Antigua and also in St. Kitts. She is a poet, songwriter, and playwright and has often used these gifts for self-expression and as a medium for sharing God's love.

She holds a Bachelor's degree in Theology and a Masters in Family Life Education. She is the wife of Rev. Algernon Lewis and mother of two young men, Yemun and Y'Mahzie Lewis. She remains passionate about serving the Lord and uses any means available to share the gospel.

Printed in the USA
CPSIA information can be obtained
at www.ICGtesting.com
LVHW092023191023
761583LV00027B/348/J